# YOU WILL
## (PROBABLY)
# SURVIVE

# LAUREN DUBOIS

# YOU WILL
## (PROBABLY)
# SURVIVE

## AND OTHER THINGS THEY DON'T
## TELL YOU ABOUT MOTHERHOOD

ALLEN&UNWIN
SYDNEY • MELBOURNE • AUCKLAND • LONDON

Allen & Unwin
83 Alexander Street
Crows Nest NSW 2065
Australia
Phone:    (61 2) 8425 0100
Email:    info@allenandunwin.com
Web:      www.allenandunwin.com

 A catalogue record for this
book is available from the
National Library of Australia

ISBN 978 1 76087 547 3

Set in 11/17 pt Syndor ITC by Midland Typesetters, Australia
Printed and bound in Australia by Griffin Press, part of Ovato

10 9 8 7 6 5 4 3 2

For my children
You made me a mum and taught me everything I know and
love about motherhood, including how hard it is to write a
whole book. With you. All over me. All of the time.

# Contents

# Preface

*In a small brown room, wallpapered with posters for meningococcal vaccinations and breastfeeding classes, a circle of women sat on green plastic chairs, cradling their brand-new babies, hoping everyone could see how well they were coping.*

*The smiles were fixed, and appearances were being kept, until the voice of one brave woman cut through.*

*'This is really hard,' she said. 'Why didn't anyone tell us it would be this* hard?'

*Her white flag was an amnesty for the group, giving us the freedom to tell the truth.*

*'Oh but they* did *tell us,' I replied. 'We just didn't* believe *them.'*

I'd been told motherhood was hard. 'Toughest job in the world!' they said.

I heard them. I believed it was hard . . . for *them.*

'It won't be like that for me,' I thought. 'I'm smart. I can do things. I'm a capable, successful woman.'

You can imagine my surprise when I learnt that being educated would mean *nothing* when it came to my parenting skills. I'm still in shock, to be honest.

My initiation into motherhood was a storm that gusted and howled at the sands of my soul—and its very first blow was to my ego.

Yelling at my little hurricane 'I HAVE A MASTER'S DEGREE!' (a super healthy thing to do) should've been a clue that I wasn't coping with the complete loss of control or my inability to succeed.

One of the first truths of parenting I learnt was: you can't study your way out of it.

Being a mother is not something you can learn from a book #irony #thanksforyourpurchase. Even though, technically, there *is* a manual for parenting. There are thousands of books and millions of internet pages. There's more information on parenting than any human being could ever digest and it still won't teach you how to actually *be* a parent.

Parenthood is one of those learn-on-the-job kinda gigs, like an apprenticeship. But it's an apprenticeship that never really ends. You're a lifelong trainee, constantly working towards, but never quite achieving full qualification.

But here's the thing: YOU WILL (probably) SURVIVE. Sure, there'll be days when you'll start saying goodbye to your loved ones, convinced the end is near, but ultimately, you'll pull through. You'll be bruised and battered, like an overripe banana sitting in the bottom of your backpack, and pieces of you might break, fall off or disappear altogether, but YOU WILL SURVIVE. Probably. You might even thrive. Maybe.

Sharing your war stories is an excellent coping technique. Please note: this *does not* mean handing out unsolicited advice. Good lord, please don't be one of those people. Those people are the ingrown toenails of the parenting world. Let's all agree: we don't tell anyone *how to* parent, but we *can* tell them our stories so they feel less alone.

So this is what I'm doing right now: letting you know some of the things you might not have been told about parenthood so that when you get there, you'll know you're not the only one going through it.

I'm also going to tell you stuff they've probably already told you, but you didn't really believe. BELIEVE ME. It's easier if you know . . .

But . . . who is 'they'?

You know! The sprawling civilisation of They! It's *all* of them. It's your mum and your sisters and your aunties and your cousins. It's your friends and your random colleague Sharon who has a sixteen-month-old child, so you know she's an expert in all areas of child rearing and she really, *really needs* you to know everything she's learnt. They are the movies and TV shows you've grown up watching.

And let's not forget the experts—the parenting experts who can never agree on a goddamn thing, and the medical professionals who have a special talent for making you feel like an idiot every time you ask a question. And, of course, there's the online world of forums, bloggers and social media where parenting is an extreme sport—a competition for likes and comments—where anonymity means everyone's a target for the sanctimummy. She's the sanctimonious mother who is absolutely perfect (in her unhumble opinion) and can't wait to tell you why you're doing it all wrong.

'They' are all the voices buzzing in your ear about parenthood. But you know what? None of them are giving you the full story.

But I will. I'm going to tell you the whole, real, glorious, uncomfortable and unforgiving truth about motherhood.

And the very first thing I want you to know is: EVERYTHING changes. Absolutely everything. Your life, your relationship, your friendships . . . *you change*. The minute a baby is placed in your arms, you start a journey of change, piece by piece, evolving until you are no longer just 'you', you are 'mum'. It's one of the most overwhelming, amazing and humbling experiences you'll ever go through, and it can be bloody sobering to realise, a few months in, that this new world of yours is so incredibly *irreversible*.

Once your child is here, you're a mother. For life.

But here's the most important thing to know, and I want you to remember it as you read this book: *most of us choose to do it all again*. We whinge and complain about how hard it is, how exhausted we are, how inadequate we feel every damn day . . . and yet every one of us will tell you it's worth it. *They're* worth it.

SO worth it.

# Part one
# Pregnancy

## or
## *What's happening to me?*

*Dear Mum-to-be,*

*Congratulations, you're pregnant! How are you feeling? Excited? Scared?*

*Don't worry, you'll be fine. Women have been doing it for thousands of years, they say! Most natural thing in the world!*

*And with those comments (often uttered by men, because gosh it's fun when men share their opinions on pregnancy, don't you think?), they've dismissed everything about creating a human that makes it such an achievement. Because growing a baby isn't just getting a big belly and feeling nauseous for a few weeks.*

*Oh, sister, no. It's a tad more involved than that.*

*Pregnancy is the most bizarre and mystifying thing your body will ever go through. And I mean that in the least terrifying way possible. I mean, sure, you might go through it skipping and laughing and rubbing that glorious belly of yours in everyone's face. That's entirely possible and I wish you all the best with that.*

*It is, however, a little more likely that your entire body will swell, transform and totally reconfigure itself to make way for the ~~parasite~~ bundle of joy invading your abdomen and pushing down on your genitalia until it feels like the whole mess could fall right out of your body.*

*Have you ever seen a picture of what your organs do while the foetus is in residence? Everything that used to fit in there perfectly is relocated, like refugees in your body. They're pushed into hostile places where they don't belong. They can't go back to where they came from because their home is now occupied and dangerous. Your liver is in your ribs, your* stomach is in your throat and your kidneys are resting on your rectum. It's a humanitarian crisis in there. Add to that: a whole human being with limbs that get stuck under ribs and stretch at your skin—and your body is an actual war zone.

That little person inside your body (yes, YOU HAVE A WHOLE PERSON INSIDE YOU) will do unspeakable things to your organs and joints; it will have you lurching from deliriously happy to murderous all in the space of five minutes; it will leave you barely able to move until you're begging for it to GET OUT. Eventually it'll tear your vagina to pieces as it forces its way out, leaving you peeing and pooing yourself like a degenerate.

Oh, sorry, love, is this making you uncomfortable? I apologise; it can be a bit confronting. But once you've had a child, it will seem bloody hilarious. No matter what sort of person you were 'before', pushing a human out of your body will gift you with a new-found shamelessness when it comes to talking about your genitals and how it all works (or doesn't work, as the case will very likely be). Fanny jokes just become funny. When your V has been to war and returned, she enjoys having a good laugh about it with her comrades, you know?

While you may know some of the technical details of what's going to happen while you're creating life, you probably don't know The Whole Story. Because people never tell you The Whole Story because The Whole Story can be a bit . . . confronting. But I reckon forewarned is forearmed, and it's better to know all of it now so you don't feel like a freak when it happens to you.

Just remember . . . you'll (probably) survive.

Love Lauren xx

# 1

# Pregnancy is a whole-body condition

I've always been fascinated with stories of women who didn't know they were pregnant. One day they trotted off to hospital with a tricky case of indigestion, and the next day they came home with an infant.

How is it physically possible to not notice the whole extra person inside your body? Even if you're lucky enough to escape the nausea, the heartburn, the fatigue and ravenous hunger, how do you explain the uppercuts to the diaphragm when your pregnancy is nearing full term and your child is desperate to get out? How do you rationalise the taser strikes to the cervix? And, more importantly, how do I get one of those pregnancies? Because they sound infinitely more pleasurable than the kind I got, which were . . . *quite noticeable.*

Although, to be fair, having an unexpected baby would actually be god-awful. I know a woman who didn't discover she was pregnant until she was nearly 30 weeks gone. I was jealous until I realised she was spectacularly short-changed. Pregnant women need the full 40 weeks to wrap their minds around the fact that their lives are about to change, irrevocably and forever.

So perhaps we should be grateful that, for most of us, pregnancy will make itself known. Really, really known. Like, you probably won't be wandering around at 36 weeks and forgetting you've got an extra body inside yours.

Here are a few things you need to know up-front:

- Pregnancy isn't something that happens to just your belly. (Ha! Wouldn't that be fun?) No. Pregnancy happens to your WHOLE body. All of the bits. There will be moments you'll feel pregnant in your earlobes. It's quite involved.
- It can affect ANYTHING. Literally anything that is new, baffling or weird over the next nine months could be pregnancy related.
- It's all weird. Your Google search history is about to get lit.
- There's no way you're leaving this situation unscathed. I'm so sorry if you thought you'd be some sort of mythical creature who'd snap back to what she was before, with a little bit of effort and the right food. Lady, *this is going to leave a mark.*

Imagine, for example, you took a balloon, blew it up to its full size and then deflated it.

Or you took a piece of paper, scrunched it into a tiny ball and then tried to flatten it out again.

Or you took a watermelon, scooped out the insides, mixed those insides with half a bottle of vodka, froze it, blended it, put it back in the watermelon skin with a bunch of other fruit and then ran over the watermelon with your car.

A little bit like that.

It might not be traumatic or dramatic. It might not even be

noticeable to the outside world, but there will be a few bits and pieces that'll never make it back to where they used to be.

Pregnancy is also a moving feast. It evolves and transforms from one month to the next so just as you settle in to one stage, things will change and you'll be thrown into a whole new hit-list of weirdness. Here's a rough timeline of what to expect:

# Weeks 1–15

Feeling like garbage. Bloated, tired, chubby, greasy-haired, nauseous porky town. No one knows you're pregnant so you have to deal with raised eyebrows and whispers as you reach for another packet of chips and undo one more button on your groaning pants. No one told you you'd just look bloated for months.

# Weeks 16–29

Pregnancy glory. You've 'popped' so you finally look pregnant and it's exactly like all the magazines told you it would be—you're in your cute tight dress, showing off your adorable little bump and your delightful new set of boobs. You are a goddess, and everyone treats you as such. Take many photos.

# Weeks 30–36

Chunky ankles, fat arse, huge boobs and pudgy arms. You're not just pregnant in your belly, you're pregnant EVERYWHERE. Is it possible to put on weight in your nose? Because yours has spread across your whole face. Your skin is seeking revenge for all the years you ignored the sunscreen. You're looking at lip-waxing kits in the chemist. Your 'cute' belly looks like a road map and GOOD GRIEF will someone turn the air-con on.

## Final 4 weeks

DANGER ZONE. Do not approach the pregnant woman. Do not talk directly to her. Do not look her in the eye.

They say pregnancy goes for nine months, but it's actually 40 weeks, which is more like ten months. But by the end, it feels like you've been pregnant for seventeen months and you want to hurt someone. (If it makes you feel any better, the second pregnancy feels like it goes for about a week and a half.)

So yeah, when you are growing a human, it's not confined to your uterus. You will be pregnant from the hair on your head to the toes on your feet. Let's have a look at some of the fun little ways your body will remind you that it is no longer *your* body, it's merely the host body for the life-sucking wonder inside it. Shall we start at the top?

## Hair

HELLO GLORIOUS HAIR! Did you know that most women stop shedding hair in pregnancy? So all the hair that usually ends up down the plughole stays on your head, and by the end of those nine months, you'll be looking all Blake Lively with your fine-ass mane.

Of course, like absolutely everything to do with pregnancy, this won't happen for everyone, so fair warning: this could be a spiteful promise of glory that never eventuates.

Side note: the luxurious hair may not be confined to your head. It can also come in thick and fast everywhere you have hair and many places you shouldn't have hair. Enjoy that.

Side side note: the hair doesn't stay. But let's leave that tragedy for the newborn section.

# Skin

Oh, the glow of pregnancy. And by glow, I mean the slick, greasy shine of your T-zone, the mottled sparkle of your skin's pigmentation, and that rosy gleam of rosacea.

Your Blake Lively hair is doing its best to distract from the crack addict skin. Pigmentation, acne, weird rashes and a flushed face will leave you feeling so #blessed.

OR it could be the best skin of your life. You never know. It's like skin roulette!

Side note: an old wives' tale says that if you have beautiful skin in pregnancy you'll be having a boy, but if your skin is shocking it's a girl because baby girls steal your beauty. Gross stereotype or not, this was actually true for me.

# Eyes

They'll want to close, a lot. Because you'll be tired. The first trimester will have you near-hysterical with how fatigued you are. New hormones, building a placenta, the drain on your vitamins and minerals; it can all leave a girl feeling a touch grumpy. Naps in the work loos become a constant temptation. Public transport leads to public snoring. You'll walk in the door from work, sit down on the couch and only wake when someone prods you and tells you to eat something or go to bed.

The second trimester is often the time this all disappears and you'll bounce around like an adorable pregnant puppy, with your tiny little bump and your glossy mane of hair, telling everyone how marvellous pregnancy is.

And then the third trimester turns up to slap your perky arse back into bed. It's not quite the same as the inexplicable fatigue of the first trimester. This exhaustion is simply because you are large and you can't sleep. It's possible you'll have to be spoken to more than once about threatening violence against people who tell you to get as much sleep as you can now 'before the baby arrives'.

## Dreams

You're not imagining it. Your dreams have become mighty effed-up. They're long, complicated, utterly disturbing and you can recall every frightening detail when you wake up. These are the kind of dreams that'll have you wondering if someone as demented as you should be allowed to bring a child into this world. If what you're growing even is a child? Maybe it's a demon sprite that possesses you at night?

It's okay. They're totally normal. I mean, the dreams aren't normal, they're seriously unnerving, but it's normal to have them during pregnancy, because hormones. (Yeah, this will be a recurring theme. It's all hormones.)

## Nose

It can become really stuffed up. Because why should breathing be easy for you?

All the mucus-producing parts of your body will go into over-drive so you could be all blocked up for quite a while. And yes, I did notice how gag-worthy the phrase 'mucus-producing parts of your body' was. Welcome to pregnancy.

Your nose might also bleed now and then. Because why not?

## Smell

The stuffy nose could be a blessing though, because the alternative is that you can breathe *and smell* through your nose, and when pregnancy turns you into an actual bloodhound, you don't want to smell anything. It's like you've never smelled smells before in your life, and the greatest tragedy is that the world smells SO BAD.

The supercharged sense of smell is apparently to help pregnant women in the wild avoid all the soft cheese and oysters or something like that, but in reality it just highlights the stench-hole we all live in. Normal people walk around like everything is fine but pregnant women know we're all living in a rancid, steaming garbage pile.

You'll discover your boss never washes his hair because you can smell it from outside his office.

You'll know what Janice had for dinner last night and, to be honest, it's probably why she's still single.

Public toilets will become a nightmare of putridity.

As an added bonus, YOU might also stink—and it's a smell that no amount of showering and/or deodorant can erase. How lovely.

## Teeth

Yes, even your teeth. Your gums are probably going to bleed. You've got so much extra blood swishing around your body, and your gums are extra sensitive so brushing your teeth is an open invitation for bloodshed.

Also, your teeth can MOVE. Some women end up getting braces after they've finished having kids because their teeth shifted so much during pregnancy. Seriously, no part of your body is safe.

## Drool

You might wake up one morning, your face all juicy and your pillow sopping wet, and desperately try to remember what you were doing last night.

Turns out, you've been drooling like a bull-mastiff. So much saliva, so little mouth control. You might want to grab a handtowel and put it on your pillow. And tell your partner not to mention a thing if he wants to continue sleeping next to you.

## Jaw

Yep, it could get all sore and out of joint. Pretty much like every joint in your body. That magical hormone relaxin—the one that helps your pelvis move and expand to fit the baby—leaches into every part of your body until you're a full-on Gumby, which can be problematic if you want to stay in one piece.

## Armpits

I'm throwing this in here because I had super itchy armpits during pregnancy. Scratched the bejesus out of them. I've never met another person who's experienced this, but I figure if it's in a book, it'll become legitimate. The secret shame of my itchy armpits is now out in the mainstream.

## Boobs

One of the first signs of pregnancy for many women will be sore boobs. This isn't period boob pain; this is next-level trauma to the chest region.

Imagine someone's taken to your boobs with a meat tenderiser, seasoned them with pepper, pan-fried them with some onions, then chewed them up and spat them back out again.

So yeah, they'll be raw. It's time to say goodbye to underwire bras, those medieval torture devices.

They'll also be huge. If yours were originally of the 'cute and pert' variety, your pregnancy boobs will be the best knockers of your life. Take dozens of photos. Rejoice in how full and how high they look. Enjoy that cleavage. Get those girls out every chance you get because people really do love a good set of melons. (If they're just for show, that is. If they're functional breasts—for, you know, feeding infants—boobs are mortifying and dangerous for the more sensitive members of society.)

If your bust was already pretty impressive, this is going to be a daunting time for you, my friend. The bosom could take over. It's lucky you're not supposed to lie on your back during pregnancy, because they might just creep up to smother you in your sleep, the sneaky little devils.

Also, fair warning: your boobs might leak as you get closer to your due date. Nothing to worry about. You'll be leaking from everywhere soon enough.

# Nipples

Remember when your nipples were all teeny tiny and cute? Ah, bless those little nips. Say goodbye. That's the end of that.

They'll grow and grow and grow and get darker and darker until half your boob is nipple. Roughly the size of a dinner plate or a nice cheese platter, right there on your chest. There's a theory that says your nipples become offensively large and dark so your baby can find them when they're born. Clever little monkeys.

# Balance

Your balance will go askew, FYI. If you're carrying all this new junk in your front it can throw everything off. Walking down stairs can become a challenge when you can't see your feet, and leaning down to look where you're stepping isn't a great idea when all your weight is there to start with.

Oh, and you might be dizzy if your blood pressure is a bit low, so a dizzy, off-balance pregnant woman is a woman who should be sitting down with her feet up, watching TV and eating snacks. In my humble opinion.

## Heartburn

Heartburn sounds a bit cute, doesn't it? Like something out of a country song. Or like your heart has popped off to Fiji for some R&R and wasn't very sun safe while playing beach volleyball.

What it actually feels like is molten lava bubbling up your oesophagus, burning great acidic holes right through your food pipe until you begin to fear your food will start seeping directly into your body cavity. You'll need to sleep sitting up because every time you lie down, you worry actual fire will leak out of your mouth.

It's unpleasant, but it's okay—you get to drink liquid chalk to calm it down. Yay.

Side note: there's an old wives' tale that says if you get heartburn, it means your baby will have a lot of hair. There was a point in my pregnancy where I feared I was about to birth a Persian cat.

## Hunger

People will snidely tell you that you're not really 'eating for two' so you don't need to gorge like an animal.

I challenge those people to take some food off a pregnant lady and see how that works out.

No, you don't need twice the amount of calories, *allegedly*. Nutritionists claim you only need a few hundred more every day to sustain the growing person inside your body.

Quite frankly, I don't know or care how many more calories you need; all I know is that at certain times in my pregnancies I would get so hungry that I would double over in pain. Like my stomach was eating itself in a quest to fill an unfillable void.

I slept with food next to my bed, and my husband would often wake to find me sitting up, eating a banana at 3 a.m.

The worst part of being hungry/hangry is right at the end of pregnancy when you're ravenous, every minute of every day, but can't eat more than a few bites because your human occupier has its feet shoved into your stomach, flattening it to a quarter of its original size. It's like a gastric bypass you didn't ask for or want. It's a hunger that can never be satisfied and it's inhumane.

## Breathing

Your womb invader can also make it really hard to breathe. That can happen when a person has two feet resting inside your diaphragm, the inconsiderate little twerp. But it can also happen in the first trimester simply because of the extra progesterone in your body. So you'll feel chubby, out of breath, sick and exhausted and you can't tell anyone about it. Have I mentioned the first trimester is the worst?

## Burping and farting

Constant.

## Nausea

I refuse to call this 'morning sickness'. What skid mark decided to make it sound like some sort of whimsical, time-limited quirk of health? It's not a morning thing; it's an all-day and all-night thing. It's like you're stuck in the worst hangover of your life for weeks and weeks and weeks on end.

What you might not know is that vomiting isn't always the worst part. The waves of nausea that stop you from speaking, moving or even thinking; this is the killer. The threat that you could throw up at any minute hangs over your head like a bucket of spew ready to tip. The 'will-I-won't-I?' is exhausting; so don't let anyone downplay your agony just because you're not physically throwing up all day.

When it finally does all come up, it can actually feel like a release. Like a sneeze that's been coming for hours. Sure, it's gross, and you'll probably wee your pants a little bit with every lurch of your stomach (and you'll almost definitely notice your toilet needs a good bleaching) but hopefully you'll get a few minutes of calm before the storm hits again.

The really twisted part about this is that for most people, it'll be worst from about six weeks until about twelve or thirteen weeks—which is traditionally the period before you've announced your pregnancy.

So you'll be stuck in work meetings wishing you could crawl under the desk with a bowl of hot chips and a pillow, dry-heaving into your handbag and willing yourself not to spew on your boss's shoes. Your colleagues will ask you if you're tired because the pasty-grey sheen of your skin is turning their stomachs, and you're forced to smile, flash your furry teeth (because brushing makes you gag) and tell them you're absolutely fine.

The quease will start to ease for some women at about twelve weeks, but most will still feel yuck until about fifteen weeks, so this is not just a first-trimester thing. Some lucky lasses will continue to hurl right up until the day they deliver. That was me #blessed.

The strangest thing is that some days you'll wake up and feel perfectly fine—and then you'll panic that something is wrong with the baby. Don't worry; you'll most likely feel deathly again the next day #grateful.

Spare a thought for any woman who experiences hyper-emesis gravidarum or HG. This is not morning sickness, and it's not nausea. It's round-the-clock head-in-toilet vomiting that often ends in hospitalisation because they simply can't keep any food or liquid down. It's dangerous, debilitating and a curse you wouldn't wish on your worst enemy. HG survivors are warriors.

# Belly

Obviously, you're going to get larger. Traditionally women aren't fond of getting a bigger gut but a baby bump is special and I hope you love it as much as I did.

The best part is: the bigger it grows, the firmer it gets. Did you hear me? SO FIRM. Like a rock. Haven't you always wanted rock-hard abs? I mean, it won't be actual abs. They'll depart as soon as your ankles do, but it's a deliciously liberating feeling to no longer worry about rolls of fat when you bend over. Sure, it's vain and superficial, but excuse me, this belly is magnificent.

Even women who've always shied away from wearing tight clothes will want to slip on a stretchy dress and flaunt that bump wherever they go. It's like all those years of being told you need to be tiny are overridden by your body's biological drive to be 'with child'. A deep, ancient part of your psyche wants to be bigger, rounder, fuller.

Not to mention, the attention you'll get from everyone else. Even if you're feeling like rubbish, most people around you will think you're a goddess. Everyone LOVES a baby bump.

Plus, never underestimate the value and novelty factor of 'The Tummy Table'. It's handier than you think.

# Bellybutton

The transformation of the bellybutton, however, is fascinating. I recommend placing bets among your family as to if/when the innie will become an outie.

Mine popped out quite early, and from then on it was like a live wire—touching it would send an electric shock straight through my body and make me feel like spewing.

So you can imagine how well I took it when complete strangers would touch my bump, inadvertently brushing against my belly-button. They may as well have pinched a nipple.

I'm happy to say no one pressed charges against me.

## Round ligament pain

Your body needs to fit a whole second body inside it, so things need to get stretchy. And that can be bloody painful.

Round ligament pain is like growing pains for your belly. Coughing, bending, picking things up, laughing too hard, turning over in bed . . . just don't do any of those things and you should be okay. Otherwise, you could get an excruciating stabbing sensation in your guts that'll have you in a total panic. (What's new?)

You might also feel that pain in your ribs as they expand to fit that kid in there. Did you know it takes up to two years for your ribs to go back to where they were before? Yep. You probably won't go back to your old bras for a while. But, honestly, who *wants* to go back to underwire?

## Linea nigra

This is the dark line that pops up on your lower tummy (often co-starring with its mate 'belly fur'). Some people say the line is there to help newborns find their way up to mum's boobs in the 'infant crawl'. (Yes, some newborns can crawl their way up mum's tummy just minutes after being born. Nature, hey?) It's basically a runway for babies. It's like lights along the aeroplane cabin, showing bubby the way to Milk Town.

Or it could just be a hormonal thing, like everything else. But that's far less exciting.

It does fade after you give birth, but it's a weird little thing—especially if you get a crooked one like I did. It's like my body was trying to throw my poor child off course.

## Stretch marks

The streeeeeetch of your skin can be particularly uncomfortable. If you've always had a pretty tight rig, your skin could stress out with the stretching sensation, making you feel sore and itchy and sensitive, like you're cracking all over. You could also be left with permanent reminders.

I'm talking about tiger stripes and battle scars. You're either going to get them or you're not. It's all a matter of genetics. It doesn't matter if you were big or small to start with and it doesn't matter how expensive that belly oil is. Literally, no potion on the planet will stop those purple, angry streaks appearing because they come from underneath the skin's surface—where no cream can reach. They will fade over time and won't be quite as purple or as angry, but they'll never completely disappear.

But keep on slathering your bump if it makes you feel better! No harm in having a silky-smooth belly. And the baby will love feeling your hands rubbing away. Yes, really, they can feel it. How freaky weird cool is that? Did you know towards the end of your pregnancy they can see light too? Shine a torch straight on your belly and see if the baby moves.

## Hips

The pressure on your hips, pelvis and general baby-making area is extreme. It's literally holding you all in.

As that relaxin pours through your body, it could entice your hips to take off on a holiday to the south of France, leaving you walking around like an 84-year-old woman.

Some women will be so rubbery they'll end up with sacroiliac joint pain and/or pelvic girdle pain—two of the most painful conditions you'll ever experience. Walking, sitting and turning over in bed will become agony. I had this and was in tears every day. Don't suffer in silence: you need a doctor or a physio and perhaps some medical support garments to help you through. Glamorous, no? But it's no joke. Some women end up using crutches or even a wheelchair at the end stages of pregnancy.

# Fanny

My goodness this is a fun one. When your vagina can no longer bear the responsibility of holding everything in, it can explode. Like a burst frankfurter turned inside out, exposing the fleshy meat inside. One day you'll realise that everything that was on the inside is now on the outside and it's twice its normal size. Don't be alarmed: it's just your vulva. Poor pet is under quite a bit of strain down there so she might swell up a bit. So if your doctor checks down there and says, 'Whoa, that's a big one!' don't be surprised or offended even though obstetricians should probably be better at hiding their shock when looking at a pregnant woman's vajayjay. If you ask me.

Oh, and varicose veins in the fanny are a real thing. FYI.

Shout out to all the discharge as well. Isn't discharge the most disgusting word in the English language? No wait, that's *moist*. Or *mucus*! Coincidence? The moist, mucus discharge is real and unrelenting. There's an ever-present gooey feeling down there. There could also be a bit of wee mixed in but, honestly, does a bit of wee make much difference?

Then there's the mucus plug. This is a fun one for your partner to research. Ask him to look it up and find out what it is so he can better understand the signs of labour. He wants to be involved, doesn't he?

Oh, and thrush! Don't forget about thrush! Honestly, it's just a good nine months of bedlam down there. Which can be tricky when you can't see it anymore.

One silver lining though: NO PERIODS! Hooray!

## Lightning crotch

You'll be walking along, having a lovely gossip with your girlfriend, taking in the warm breeze, enjoying the bird calls in the air, when BAM! Lightning crotch.

All the nerves jangling around near your cervix are in a right state of panic as they get ready to evict the person inside you. As they fuss about, they might fire off stray electrical pulses that feel like a bolt of electricity shooting straight up your clacker. It's like being zapped in the hoo-ha with a cattle prod. It's like you've been fanny-punched by an invisible imp.

It's quick, it's devastating, it's over, and you're back to your day. Pregnancy is fun, no?

## Wee

I once went on a water binge because I read that drinking three to four litres of water a day would make me look ten years younger. I basically spent a week on the toilet, like a hose with a hole in it. (I didn't look ten years younger, by the way. *Don't try this.*)

Pregnancy is a similar experience. You'll be about five weeks pregnant and all of a sudden you need to wee. All. The. Time. You won't get through two hours of sleep before your bladder wakes you up and reminds you to go. With all the extra blood flowing through your kidneys, you'll start pumping out about twenty-five per cent more wee than normal. Some days it'll feel like there's no end to the amount of fluid your body can produce.

Then, when the baby starts to grow, it'll start kicking your bladder for sport. This is an enjoyable way to wet yourself.

Then, when the baby gets really big, it'll sleep with its rock-melon head snuggled into your bladder, reducing it from about the size of a teacup to the size of a tablespoon. When you realise you need to go to the toilet, you'd better already be inside the bathroom, otherwise it's too late. You're weeing.

## Constipation

On the other hand, pooing will stop, so that's something.

## Haemorrhoids

All of that straining to poo could leave you with a darling string of haemorrhoids, and the kicker is that they mightn't ever leave. There's just so much pressure down there, and with all the extra blood flow it's just a throbbing, protruding vein waiting to happen.

Giving birth does not help this situation, FYI.

## Sweat

You'll also be super sweaty, by the way. Just everywhere, and especially at night. Pregnancy will make you hot. So very hot. And not hot in the 'Check me out!' way; hot in the 'I hate everyone' way.

Please spare a thought for all women who planned their pregnancies so poorly that they are eight months gone in the depths of summer. It's a hot, sweaty, swollen mess and everyone in their vicinity will suffer because of it.

# Leg cramps

In a further attempt to make sure you don't sleep ever again, your body will periodically wake you up with crippling leg cramps. The ones where your toes curl up uncontrollably and you need to get out of bed and stand on your leg to force it to remember how to be a leg and not a burning rod of fire and pain.

# Feet

Your feet might grow. Isn't that fun? I'm not just talking about the swelling in your ankles and feet, which can also happen (and can be a sign of pre-eclampsia or high blood pressure and should be checked out by your doctor). I'm talking about the actual bones in your feet spreading out as the ligaments loosen up.

A lot of women will end up wearing a larger shoe size because of their pregnancy. And it's usually permanent. New shoe wardrobe, yay!

Yep, having a baby can affect your whole body, from the very tips of your hair down to the bones in your feet. When you're pregnant, YOU are pregnant. Not just your belly—the whole shebang. All of it. SO VERY PREGNANT.

# 2

# You create life

Yes, that all sounds like a lot—and it is—but do you even understand the kind of *currency* this gives you for the rest of your life?

YOU ARE GROWING A PERSON INSIDE YOUR BODY, like some sort of creature from science fiction. It's straight-up witchcraft, what you've done. Forevermore when someone (i.e. your partner) tries to tell you about something incredible they just did, you can smile and nod and tell them they're very clever, and then sweetly enquire if they, by chance, grew a whole human inside their body. No? I didn't think so.

From a couple of cells, you've grown a heart, a spine, a liver, legs and arms. A WHOLE PERSON. I'm not sure it's possible to ever fully grasp the amazingness of pregnancy. Never again in your life will you accomplish so much in a day. (What did I do today? Oh, not much . . . just grew a pair of eyeballs. What about you?)

You know when you see a pregnant woman gazing off into

the distance, smiling like a spacey, round Buddha, and you assume she's having a brain freeze of some sort? That's not a brain freeze. She's sitting there thinking, 'Holy shitballs! I am an ancient vessel, built for magic, growing a person who will one day breathe and walk and talk and probably end up running the country because I can just feel her genius developing as I sit here. Because she's, you know, INSIDE ME RIGHT NOW. Because I am a woman and I grow people. Why aren't women in charge of everything? We CREATE LIFE! We're incredible!'

Those spacey, 'I'm magic' moments will help you through the 'Oh my god, my vagina is about to fall off' moments. Because you *are* magic. Trust me.

# 3

# Baby brain is real

You might have two brains inside you, but you will feel dumber than ever.

Baby brain is how Mother Nature lures us back for more children because when you have tofu for a brain, you tend to forget all the atrocities of pregnancy and gladly come back for a second round. And so the human race lives on to fight another day.

To be fair, baby brain is quite lovely. It's like nature's valium. Who are the happiest people in the world? Yep, dumb people, bless them. Because they don't know enough about anything to be angry about it. Embrace this new-found idiocy and enjoy it while it lasts, you vague little pelican.

You'll drift through your days, having a little giggle at all the silly shenanigans happening around you. You'll crack an egg into your toaster; you'll try and start your car with your phone; you'll tell your obstetrician your name is Rhonda when it's actually Bethany; you'll brush your teeth with moisturiser.

The fun part is that nobody can be mad at you or the trail of destruction you've left in your wake because YOU GREW A LIVER TODAY, OKAY? That's hard work.

We need to be kind to pregnant people. A pregnant person is not like a normal person. She's like a normal person PLUS a pregnant person. So she needs to think about, and deal with, all the normal people stuff she does every day, AND she needs to think about all the 'growing a human' stuff as well. It's an awful lot for the brain to take on. It's inevitable that some things are going to fall out the sides. And when you're trying to figure out if that weird pain in your groin is normal or not, it's really too much to be able to concentrate on Barry's presentation at work as well. Sort yourself out, Barry.

There will also be so many questions swimming around in there. SO MANY QUESTIONS. Can I eat that raw avocado? What is a cooked avocado? Can I eat a cooked prawn? Should I still be using deodorant? Is that how Stuart really smells or is that my pregnancy nose? Should I feel like I need to burp all the time? Why is Gavin looking at me like that? Is it because my boobs are almost touching my chin? Will my boobs stay like that? Why is my husband so irritating? Has he always been this irritating or am I just noticing it now?

A word of warning: baby brain might linger for a long time after the baby arrives.

Bonus tip: baby brain is the BEST excuse to be lazy and forgetful. Forgot to call your mum back? Whoops! Silly me, being so forgetful these days. Didn't get that thing at the shops your bloke wanted you to get? Yikes, I totally spaced out—this baby brain is intense!

In fact, pregnancy is a brilliant excuse for all sorts of things. I can't think of anything you *can't* blame on your pregnancy:

- No, sorry, I can't pick up that thing because I'm pregnant.
- Oh goodness, no, I couldn't *possibly* stand up right now—can't you see I'm pregnant?

- Oh, your uncle's retirement party? It's right in the middle of my scheduled nap, which the doctor says I must stick to because the baby needs it.
- Oh, you wanted that last piece of cake? So sorry, I'm going to have to step in here, because I'm *pregnant*. The baby needs it.
- Clean out the kitty litter? Couldn't possibly! It'll hurt the baby!
- Whoops, did I just call that man a horse-whipping suck boy? Goodness me, these pregnancy hormones have got me all aflutter!

People will forgive you for almost everything, so it's your responsibility to use and abuse your power for as long as you've got it. Enjoy.

# 4

# The rules of announcement

Apparently, women aren't allowed to tell anyone they're pregnant until they're at least twelve weeks into their pregnancy. This seems to be a self-imposed rule we've put in place to safeguard ourselves in case of miscarriage. We don't want to jinx anything, and we reason that if we were to miscarry our baby, at least we didn't tell anyone, so it wasn't really real anyway.

Isn't that a lovely way to make sure you suffer in silence? Because, apparently, miscarriage is so taboo that we shouldn't ever talk about it, or expect love and support through it?

The first twelve weeks can be the hardest time of pregnancy, and you're expected to do it alone. You might feel sick as a dog and so exhausted you can barely keep your eyes open. You don't have the cute bump to feel excited about, you can't feel the baby move, you need to wee all the time, and no one knows why you won't leave your home at night anymore.

You're consumed with ALL THE QUESTIONS and you just want to bloody talk to someone about it because it's the only thing you can think about, but instead you have to sit there and pretend you're interested in Debbie's sister's gall bladder surgery while you fake drinking a champers so no one will suspect you're knocked up.

So I fully support your right to tell anyone and everyone about your pregnancy whenever you feel like it. Because telling people takes it from the surreal to the SO VERY REAL and that can be a massive relief.

Plus, telling people is when you can officially GET EXCITED. There's nothing like announcing to your family and friends that there's going to be a mini-you arriving soon, and seeing their faces light up with joy. It's no longer just your tiny little secret—it's every-one's baby and they can't wait.

# 5

# Opinions and advice: part 1

Of course, announcing your pregnancy means you'll be inundated with the views of every woman, man, dog and cockatoo in earshot. They NEED you to know what they think about your decision to procreate. Somewhere, deep inside our psyche, we still believe we're part of the 'village' that raises everyone else's children, and let me tell you: the village idiot takes this more seriously than anyone. Be prepared.

There's an unholy trinity of opinionated people who will shower you with their 'wisdom':

Men

People Without Kids

Old People

Men who ask questions like 'are you going to give birth naturally?' need to have a basketball inflated in their rectum. Seeing as they'd like to know and understand all the gory details.

Remember, just because some men feel like your pregnancy gives them the green light to start asking intimate and inappropriate questions about your body and your plans for parenthood, it does not mean you need to answer them. You can, however, invite them to go and make love to a cactus. But say it nicely. Men like this are often surprisingly sensitive to the opinions of others #irony.

Then there are the People Without Kids who love an opportunity to dish out advice to expectant parents because they have a nephew or they used to babysit so they know *exactly* what it's going to be like for you. But knowing how to change a nappy is not quite the same as the mental, emotional and physical challenges of being a new parent. Smile, nod and suggest they start up an Instagram account with all of their parenting advice.

Let's not forget the Old People—bless their hearts—who think they know all there is to know about having a baby because they had eight kids. Back in the 1960s. When housewives popped a valium before school pick-up every day.

These are the sweet old dears who'll tell you newborns should be having orange juice in their bottles and if you want them to go to sleep you should just dip their dummies in some brandy and it'll knock them out cold. They'll tell you to not pick up a crying baby because you'll spoil them, but a snappy slap to the thigh will sort those tears right out.

It's not their fault; that's just how things were done back then. But we've all learnt a few things in the last 50 years.

For now, talking to your doctor and sharing stories with fellow pregnant women is your safe place. All the information and opinions can start to be really overwhelming, so sometimes you'll want to crawl into a cave with some noise-cancelling headphones and just hum it out for a while. It's not a bad idea, to be honest.

# 6

# The great gender debate

Everyone wants to know 'what' you're having. Is it a girl or a boy? If you don't know what you're having, complete strangers will gladly guess for you.

Carrying high? It's a girl.

Wide bum? It's a boy!

Look like a haggard drug addict with acne and bags under your eyes? Definitely a girl.

The odds are really good for them, too. It's a fifty-fifty chance they'll get it right.

They'll want to know if you have a preference: 'What are you hoping for, love?'

'Oh, you know, just hoping it doesn't have a tail.'

If you do know what you're having, you're also going to cop some opinions. These opinions will often come from people who have no role in your life whatsoever. June at the supermarket check-out. Mark the pharmacist. The balding lady who sits at the bus stop all day. These are the people who will share their disappointment that you're not having the little girl they really wanted you to have, or will offer their condolences to your husband who must be devastated he's not getting 'his heir'.

These opinions become even more voracious for your second child. If you produce anything other than a pigeon pair—one for mum and one for dad—people will struggle to keep their disappointment to themselves. Because the balding lady at the bus stop had her heart set on you getting a little girl and you went and fell pregnant with another boy! The shame of it.

If you dare produce a third child of the same gender, people will straight-up weep for you. Having a beautiful baby just isn't enough for some people.

# 7

# The magic bump

They might have their opinions but most people mean well because, almost without exception, people love pregnant women. Apart from the odd knob-jockey on public transport, you'll find that most people—friends, family, colleagues and random strangers on the street—will smile when they see you waddle past.

People can feel the magic radiating off pregnant women. They want to be near them, they want to talk about babies with them, they want to capture some of that goddess and rub it all over themselves. Pregnant women are fascinating creatures who literally have two heads—part circus sideshow, part natural wonder.

Pregnant women *are* special. It's a truly extraordinary time in your life when you're walking around with that bump, suddenly noticing all the other pregnant women on the street, sharing secret smiles with them because you're all in this together.

You only get a few chances in your life to be pregnant. (Unless you're one of those reality show families with 28 children.) Most women will be pregnant one, two or maybe three times in their life. People want to celebrate it with you.

# 8

# You can't eat things

Every year they add some more things to the list of Stuff Pregnant Women Can't Eat. Eventually it's going to become a list of Stuff Pregnant Women *Can* Eat and the list will be:

- filtered water
- spinach (important for folic acid but make sure it's washed and rinsed at least seven times, and definitely never eat pre-packaged spinach or anything from a salad bar).

And that's it.

Pretty much everything else poses some sort of risk to the baby because we live in a cesspool of filth and disease. It's remarkable that any of us survive, what with this willy-nilly consumption of gooey eggs and soft cheeses.

Let's not even start on all the dangers of sugar and carbs. If they're not going to kill you and your baby, they're definitely going to change the epigenetics of your foetus, so while you're sitting there eating your way through a box of meringues, you are laying the foundation stones for a life of crime and despair for your unborn child.

Suddenly, every event you go to will feature a raw seafood and champagne bar. All your friends will start ordering poached eggs. Work will lay out a deli meat platter for your baby shower. It will seem like everyone you know will forget you can't eat soft cheese and they will offer it to you every four minutes until the baby is born and then you will never be offered brie again in your life. Are they trying to break you?

It's like no one knows or cares that you're pregnant and you can't eat anything anymore.

But, if you're feeling a little overlooked, all you have to do is pick up a cup of coffee and see how many people suddenly care what you're putting into your body.

Of course, everyone wants to know about your cravings. Pickles and ice cream, right? Is your poor husband being sent out in the dead of night to buy spicy chicken wings? Are you one of those people out in the backyard eating soil, or spooning detergent into your mouth?

Sadly, not everyone gets cravings, which can be a damn shame if you were looking forward to munching on dirt.

# 9

# Attacked from within

Every woman dreams about those first baby kicks. It's magical when you feel those little flutters, like a kiss from an angel in your womb. Okay, in reality it feels like you're about to fart, but nevertheless it's an amazing moment when you finally understand there's a real baby with arms and legs growing inside your belly.

For a little while, you'll be the only one who can feel those tickles; it's like a secret code between you and your baby. Those little wiggles are your baby's way of saying, *Hello, Mummy!* It's a special meeting between the two of you—for the first time.

Fast-forward a couple of months and those sweet movements become a little less romantic. When people ask what it feels like, there's only one answer: it feels EXACTLY how you think it would feel to have a human being trapped inside your body, trying to get out.

What starts out as gas bubbles turns into roundhouse kicks to the liver, and coward punches to the diaphragm that can literally knock the wind out of you, mid-sentence.

You will lie awake at night, being assaulted from within, wondering if your baby actually hates you. You'll start to panic that if they're awake and raging at 2 a.m. every day, will they keep to the same schedule on the outside? I can tell you: the answer is yes.

Did you know you'll also be able to feel the baby's hiccups? Yep, your little rascal loves, loves, *loves* to gulp that amniotic fluid, which is really just a sack of his own waste products. Yummy. So, as your little possum learns how to swallow, he'll get hiccups now and then. Or every bloody day. It's not annoying *at all*. It's so cute how it feels like your baby has an unfortunate tic that means you'll feel a steady bump every few seconds FOREVER. So fun. So cute. Not irritating at ALL.

Towards the end of your pregnancy, your baby will start to run out of room and will take it out on you by trying to stretch its little limbs. It'll push and roll under your skin; tiny feet, hands and skull jutting out of your gut in the most nauseating way. You'll look at your undulating belly, feeling every organ being battered from within and you'll know exactly how they came up with that scene in *Alien*.

While all of this sounds bizarre, nothing, not one thing, compares to the sensation of having a small mammal scratch at your cervix with their razor-sharp claws, in a bid for freedom. You heard me.

# 10

# The full-time job of pregnancy

It's not just a matter of falling pregnant, waiting nine months and then popping that kid out: being pregnant can feel like a full-time job.

You'll have appointments and check-ups and shopping expeditions and more appointments and hospital tours and cervical cleansing to get done.

(Kidding. Cervical cleansing is not a thing. Actually, it probably is. In fact, now I think of it, there's probably someone out there making an excellent living out of cleansing cervixes.)

Cervixes aside, you'll find your nights and weekends will become consumed with 'prepping for the baby'.

This includes researching baby products like you're buying a new car. The pram, in particular, will feel like the most significant decision of your life. Do you go prestige or budget? What sort of suspension does it have? Does it have ABS brakes? Can we get that one with the leather trim? Do we go for light and sporty or should we invest in a four-wheel drive?

This is an excellent task to delegate to the unpregnant one in the relationship. A spreadsheet listing the pros and cons of all necessary baby items would be a good start thank you very much, my love.

For something so tiny, this baby is already demanding most of your time. That's going to become their trademark, by the way. Consider this the trailer for the blockbuster: COMING SOON.

# 11

# Naming your child

Of all the decisions you'll need to make before your child's arrival, choosing a name will be the most important.

Will you co-sleep? Will you breastfeed? Will co-sleeping and breastfeeding make your child a narcissistic sociopath? Will you let them cry it out? Will letting them cry it out give your baby a lifelong gaming addiction?

Forget it all. None of it's important. Your kid'll be fine. Probably.

But giving your child the wrong name could be a devastating mistake. Of course, it is absolutely *your* choice. This is your child; you can name it whatever you like. It won't affect you in the least. Your little Mg'winni Bear, however, will crawl through her childhood in shame and embarrassment until she turns eighteen and changes her name to Jane.

It's not an easy task either. You never realise how many people you hate until you try and find a name for your baby.

Here are some foolproof ways to help you choose a name that won't make your offspring a social pariah:

# Imagine them as prime minister

You'll never see the headline 'Wizdom has been elected prime minister'. You need to be able to take your PM (semi-) seriously. Give your child a fighting chance.

# Visualise their job applications

Even if you don't have aspirations for your child to run the country, I'm assuming you want them to be employed at some point in their life.

Imagine a recruiter flicking through job applications. Do they stop at the application of Glittyr Faery or do they keep going? And what do *you* think the job opportunities for Sparrkyl Dusst are? Where's ol' Sparrkyl D headed in life?

# Yell it loud and bogan

You're going to need to say this name a lot. How does it sound when you scream it across the playground in your best bogan?

'FERRARI-LEEEEE! Get here NOW!'

Seriously, get your list of baby names and start screaming them out. You'll cull that list quick smart.

# Pretend they're your boss

Does the name command respect? Would you be able to take direction from a person called Peace Pear Moonharvest? Can you imagine someone saying, 'Oh bloody hell, Miaow Boo wants me to stay back tonight to finish that report'?

# Do the kindergarten spelling test

When you're feeling creative and decide to throw a bunch of letters together to invent that unique one-of-a-kind name for your little darling, just try and give some thought to that poor child once they hit school.

Try to imagine those pudgy little fingers wrapped around the HB pencil, trying their damnedest to spell out Zynfendanee. It's just mean.

# Can anyone else spell it?

You might like to give your child that extra edge by giving them a normal name with 'innovative' spelling. For the love of all that's good and holy, please spell your child's name correctly.

Don't condemn your child to a life of saying, 'No, it's Catherine with an X' or 'That's Jayden with an H' or 'It's Tiffany with three I's'.

I mean, my name is Lauren, which is probably one of the most common names in the history of the world, and I still need to spell my name for some people. So spare a thought for Whendhi and Djohnn.

Same goes for kids with names that are spelled correctly but pronounced creatively. If you spell your child's name 'Steven', I will call him Steven, and you can't get angry because I haven't guessed it's pronounced Steffahn.

# Take the schoolyard challenge

As your final step, ask a teenage boy for his opinion. Challenge him to do his worst with the name, as if he'd just encountered little Quinoa in the playground. (If only the parents of Drew Peacock had done this.)

# 12

# Don't mess with the pregnant lady

Trifling with a pregnant lady is a fool's errand. Only the dimmest of dimwits would challenge a woman who is growing a second spine right now.

It's like trying to defuse a bomb. Sure, you might cut the right wire, and everything will be calm and the world will be at peace.

Or you could cut the wrong wire and you will end up with no face.

A lady with a baby in the tummy is a lady who might not be feeling quite like herself.

The stone-cold bitch can turn into a bleeding heart who stays back at work every night to help the cleaning lady because she's just working *so* hard to take care of her family and it's not right that she has to do it alone.

The strong, confident woman is now the chick in the corner sobbing her heart out because the cafe ran out of banana bread and why is everything just so hard now?

The sweet, mild-mannered lass is now suddenly leaping out of her car to launch a stinging, foul-mouthed assault on the man who's taking too long to fill up his car with petrol. F#@&ing f#@&er!

The loved-up newlywed could scare herself with how violently she loathes her husband when he eats that way. How has she never noticed it before? How can she possibly raise a child with this animal? It's all been such a colossal mistake.

You might become emotional over the oddest things. Not being able to bend over because of the basketball stuck to your front. Not being able to squeeze through tight spots because you can't squash that tummy in. Not being able to see your fanny anymore. So many fun things to cry about!

It's okay, darling, you're just pregnant. You're not losing your mind. It's just taking a short break. Not sure when it'll come back. Maybe after the baby arrives, maybe not. Hard to tell. But you'll be okay. I think.

Side note: you might not become a pregnant sex kitten either. This is really only upsetting for all the partners out there who seem to know one 'fact' about pregnancy: 'She'll get horny'. Sorry to prick your bubble, fellas (see what I did there?) but some women will swing the opposite way, and the suggestion of a quick shag will make her want to hurt you.

# 13

# You don't have to love the baby yet

I've seen approximately 47 movies and TV shows where a pregnant woman offers her own life to save that of her unborn baby because the love she has for her child is already that powerful. Her husband tearfully begs her to reconsider, and the medical team will inevitably figure out a way to save them both but it's touch-and-go for a while there.

Apparently, women must feel a spiritual connection to this little creature before the two of them have even met. Which can make you feel like a heartless shell of a human when you look down at your undulating gut and feel . . . nothing.

You've heard the heartbeat, and that was great and all, but you didn't feel the waves of emotion so many other women seem to feel.

You've bought the teeny-tiny onesies and itty-bitty baby socks, and your heart didn't explode even a little bit.

Breathless women beseech you to tell them how EXCITED YOU ARE and you smile and nod and promise them you are over the moon. You wouldn't want to let them down.

Just quietly, you're completely nonplussed about the whole thing, and every time you see a leg jut out from your abdomen, you think, 'Oh hey there, you. Would you mind *not*?'

You're like flatmates, sharing the same space but not necessarily eager to spend the rest of your lives together. You don't really know anything about each other yet. I mean, you know she likes to drink her own piss, she's about the size of a papaya, and she's got a good stretching routine going on every day at 4 a.m., but apart from that you're strangers.

It's okay. You don't have to lay down your life if you don't want to. Sharing a blood supply doesn't make everyone woozy with joy. Sometimes you need to meet face-to-face before you realise you're soulmates.

# 14

# But you will (probably) like your baby, eventually

When all you've got to go on is other people's kids, it can be terrifying to think of having one of your own.

You spend one afternoon with someone else's toddler and you're suddenly choking on the fear that you've made a grave mistake.

Let me reassure you. There's an excellent chance you will like your own child. Even if you genuinely despise other people's children, your own child won't be as irritating, I promise.

I mean, don't get me wrong, your child will be irritating. Like, seriously irritating and frustrating and exasperating. But it'll be fine; you'll still really like them because they'll be yours.

It's partly biology and partly training—as in, you train intensively in preparation for a toddler. You get an exceptionally edible newborn, and the magic of their tiny head ensnares you into a lifetime of hopeless love.

Then they become cuter and cuter until you feel like you might burst with the adoration of your own production, and then they start to become a bit . . . tricky. They start to move and talk and defy you and destroy everything you possess, and they become slightly less likeable, but it's okay because the love is stronger than ever.

And then they become utter flogs and kick and spit and throw stuff and they do it all in public just to rub the humiliation of parental failure in, but it's still okay because they're yours and you get the good stuff as well as the bad. Mostly you'll be fine because the foul behaviour is incremental and you'll build up a tolerance for it. There's a reason you don't suddenly get lumped with a two year old.

So don't worry if other people's kids make your skin crawl. Kids are like farts—you never really mind your own.

# 15

# The horrible beautiful

Pregnancy is beautiful. Those women with their cute little bumps and glossy hair tell us so. Pregnant women smile a lot, and they caress their bumps, and they glow with the light of life burning inside. It's truly a sight to behold.

Pregnancy can also be a horror show of cankles, bloating, acne, and boobs that become so large they end up squashed into one long sausage boob you have to tuck under your armpits.

Some women will feel like the most beautiful versions of themselves, while others will feel the worst they've ever felt. It's an unfair lottery and you never know what you're going to get.

The hardest part is you're not allowed to complain about it, especially if you've worked hard to fall pregnant.

Women who've undergone fertility treatment or who've experienced multiple miscarriages along the way are supposed to be grateful. They're supposed to be so overjoyed about the impending arrival of their desperately wanted baby that any sign of *ungrate-fulness* is pounced on.

It doesn't matter how much you wanted this baby. It doesn't matter if you've tried for years and years to fall pregnant. The *wanting* doesn't erase the physical toll pregnancy can take.

All women can feel huge and disgusting and impatient for it all to be over and done with. It doesn't mean you don't want your baby. It doesn't mean you won't love that child when it arrives. It just means that pregnancy can be really rough.

It can also be the loveliest time of your life as you cherish how lucky you are to be a woman, experiencing the miracle of creation, holding your future in your womb, feeling the joy of anticipation.

You could be over the moon, or you could feel like a bag of compost. Neither is the 'right' way to be.

# 16

# It's okay to be scared

Pregnancy can also be mentally exhausting. There's this idea that you should be filled with joy at every moment. The glow should start deep in your womb and radiate out of your body, casting a halo of light and love around you, because you are carrying a miracle inside. It's what you were made to do and you're so #grateful to be able to do it #glowing.

Except when it isn't all bluebirds and sunbeams. Pregnancy can be nightmares and panic attacks. For the first time in your life, you're painfully aware that your future is entirely out of your control.

You don't know if your baby will be healthy. You don't know if the birth will go smoothly. And what if you hate motherhood? What if you resent this tiny alien creature for changing everything? What if it all goes wrong?

You're not crazy for thinking these things. They're all possible. You're not being melodramatic or silly; you're being realistic. You're on a path you can't get off, and that can be an overwhelming thought for anyone to wrap their mind around.

I can't tell you not to be scared. I can't tell you everything will be okay. I can't even tell you that the fears go away when the baby arrives.

I *can* tell you that we *all* worry. We all get ourselves worked up now and then. This is the beginning of many, many years of scary thoughts and consuming fear. This is motherhood. You're one of us now.

YOU WILL SURVIVE.

# 17

# Antenatal anxiety

If those worries start to become constant or stop you from getting on with your day, though, it might be something more than normal pregnancy stuff.

Up to one in ten women will experience anxiety or depression during pregnancy. One in twenty men will suffer from it too.

The fear of what's coming, the doubts over all your decisions and the worries about something going wrong can be paralysing, and it's important to talk to someone about it because you don't need to feel that way.

Pregnancy may not be a joyous, non-stop carnival of love and joy but it shouldn't be all-consuming darkness either. If you can't see any light at the end of the tunnel, it's time to let someone know so you can climb out of that hole. You deserve to have some peace.

# 18

# Tired begins now

You haven't had your baby yet, but the obsession with sleep has already begun. People will start telling you to go to bed immediately and get as much sleep as humanly possible before the baby arrives because—in case you haven't heard—babies are not excellent at sleeping.

They say this as if sleep is currency and you can save it up like the Barefoot Investor of Slumber, hour by hour, in a little safe, and when the baby is cluster-feeding (we'll get to that later), and you've had fourteen and a half minutes' sleep in three days, you can just withdraw a few hours from the sleep bank and you'll feel fresh as a milkmaid.

It doesn't work that way, my friend. You could never in your life accrue the number of hours you'll lose. It will make zero difference. And here's another thing no one seems to acknowledge: PREGNANT PEOPLE DON'T SLEEP EITHER.

The first trimester will be gross and sore and sick, and sleeping will be all you want to do, but it never feels like enough and the need to pee every hour continues through the night as well.

The second trimester feels a bit better, and your body starts to feel less poisoned but the heartburn sets in and the baby starts to kick, and you're not allowed to sleep on your back because of blood flow to your heart, so things are getting uncomfortable.

The third trimester feels like you've got a suckling pig strapped to your front and you can't bend or roll, so sleeping means you're sitting up with your eyes closed with 87 cushions carefully placed around you in an intricate and wondrous pattern, but you never actually sleep so really you're just resting your eyes.

Any time you do manage to fall asleep, you'll be assaulted with dreams so unnerving you worry for yourself because surely a normal person wouldn't be able to conjure up things that sick and depraved.

Which actually sucks so much more than you think because you will be tired, my girl. So damn tired. You will want to nap at your desk at work. You will nap at the dinner table. You will nap while getting your hair cut. Any sort of inactivity will make you want to nap.

So good luck with that!

# 19

# Oh, the plans

The most joyous part of pregnancy is imagining what sort of parent you're going to be and what sort of kid you'll be raising. You'll look around at other parents doing awful things like letting their kids watch iPads at cafes and feeding them hot chips, and you'll smile at your partner, knowing you'll never, ever do anything like that because you'll be a GOOD parent.

That's so cute. Keep doing that. There's no need for your bubble to burst while the child is still inside. Make ALL the plans, you sweet little pickle. You won't even remember them anyway, so I'm not going to stop you.

Here are some fun things you'll tell yourself during pregnancy:

- I'll still prioritise my relationship. We'll do date nights when we don't talk about the baby.
- I'll still use my gym membership.

- My child will only eat homemade organic food. No sugar or junk food for *my* child.
- I will birth my child naturally and without pain relief.
- I'll still be 'me', and I'll make time to catch up with my girlfriends.
- My life won't revolve around my baby. My baby will simply fit in with my life.
- I won't spam people with baby photos.
- Babies don't need a lot of stuff. We can just get the basics.
- The love we have for our baby will bring my partner and me closer together.
- I won't be a yelling mum. I will have patience.
- I won't be tired because I'll sleep when the baby sleeps. Newborns sleep for sixteen hours a day! That's plenty!
- I won't talk about my baby 24/7. I will still think about world affairs and other people.
- I won't let myself go. I will still wear make-up, jeans and heels every day.
- I will never think bad things about my child or wish they'd simply shut up for two minutes.

You might also have some grand plans for your child, like:

- My baby will sleep because I'll set up a foolproof routine.
- My children will never be dirty or wear ugly, gaudy clothes.
- My children will eat everything I put in front of them because there will be no other options.
- My children won't run the household. They will obey me.
- My children won't watch any screens. Ever. Forever. The TV will never be a babysitter.
- My children won't know how to get into my phone.

- My children will go to bed a bit later so we can all sleep in in the morning.

I'm not saying these things *won't* happen—I'd never ruin your dreams like that! I'm just saying: good luck, lovely. I do hope you get your unicorn baby.

# 20

# You're not fat, you're pregnant

There are two ways it can go when you're hugely pregnant.

You can feel like an ultra-feminine goddess. Never have you been more confident in your body!

Or you can feel like a dugong.

There's really no in-between.

And it's not like anyone will let you forget it. Pregnancy is like that big pimple on your face everyone insists on pointing out. You know it's there, you own a mirror, but people can't help but tell you what you look like. Just in case you hadn't realised there was a HUMAN BEING inside your body. Every step you take is another reminder of how very large you are, so there's really no need for everyone to point, stare and laugh.

But people see a pregnant woman and their normal sense of what is and isn't appropriate to say flies out the window.

Some women will be able to laugh it off, but some (most) women don't enjoy being told they're fat (shock), even if it's a 'lighthearted' joke. Not because they're sensitive, but because they're dealing with a rapidly changing body they don't even recognise anymore, and that can be confronting.

That 'lighthearted' joke doesn't sound so funny when you feel like a freak show and you've realised your body will NEVER be the same. Even if you lose every last kilo, your boobs will change, those stretch marks will never completely disappear, your pelvic floor will be a constant, faulty reminder. You've only just realised you wasted years worrying about your body when you should have been strutting around 24/7 in hotpants because everything was SO tight and young.

But if your belly is teeny, people will carry on like there's something wrong with you or your baby, and it can make you feel worried and stressed, like you've failed before you've even begun.

Sometimes the comments from people are easier to deal with when you've got a few comebacks ready to go.

If you are genuinely upset, you can always try, 'I find that really hurtful' because it's terribly effective in shutting people down.

My preferred technique, however, is to smile (genuinely) and to say thank you. 'Oh, I'm enormous? THANK YOU SO MUCH! I feel like a million bucks!'

Some other suggestions:

*You sure you're not having twins?*
Jinx! I was just about to say the same thing to you!

*Jeez, you got huge!*
I see you're loving being the skinny one for a change. Good for you!

*You must be due any minute!*
True, true … maybe you should take a step back before my waters break all over your cheap shoes.

*Somebody call SeaWorld—we've got a beached whale here!*
Yeah, and I'm a killer whale, so be quiet before I eat you.


*Hello, fatty!*
Eat a penis, mate.


Here's the thing, though: there may well come a time when you stare down at your enormous belly and realise how very much you love it. It's like a beautiful signpost telling people to treat you like bone china. People will part like the Red Sea when they see you coming and you might even start to enjoy everyone making a fuss over you.

And if anyone DOESN'T treat you like the goddess you are, like that jizz stain who won't offer you his seat on the bus? Well you might find you suddenly have the confidence to walk up, stick that glorious belly right in his face and let it gently nudge his forehead with every sway of the bus.

There's also this thing where people will touch your belly. It's not exactly clear why they do this. It's usually elderly people, and I think they're hoping the miracle of life will rub off on their hands. Which is all well and good, but DON'T TOUCH ME, STRANGE LADY AT THE CHECK-OUT.

You could slap their hand away, you could ask them to stop, you could give them a death stare, but by far the most effective method is to rub their stomach back.

You have no idea how many bellies I rubbed during my pregnancies. It's funny how offended people are when you touch their un-pregnant stomach. *Like, why would you touch me right now?* Oh, I don't know, because you're touching me?

See how that works?

# 21

# Nesting

You might feel like a hippo, and every movement is painful, but there will come a time right at the end where nothing will stop you getting down onto your hands and knees to scrub that filthy floor of yours.

You simply can't bring your baby home to this scum-palace. What would he think? Those skirting boards are shameful. Your wardrobe also needs to be sorted out *tout suite*. There's just no excuse for that flea-pit.

Then you'll become frantic about all the things that need to be finished before the baby arrives. You need to get your hair done, and your eyebrows. You've never done your nails before, but you can't imagine meeting your baby with those naked stumps.

You should also put all your babymoon photos into an album. And maybe you should start writing thank you notes now in preparation for all the baby gifts.

Basically, you'll try to tick everything off any to-do list that's ever existed in your life. It's actually not a bad idea.

# 22

# The nursery

Getting your baby's nursery ready is one of the most joyful things you'll ever do. Buying all the teeny things is irresistible. Preparing for this mini house guest, folding all those little clothes, imagining what she'll look like in that tiny crib. It's permission to dream about your life 'after'.

There are so many things you need to do when you're pregnant that you can lose sight of The Baby. You're preparing your body and thinking about the birth but the real show is The Baby. And getting that nursery ready, filling the bookshelf, folding the little singlets . . . this is when you let yourself think about holding your child in your arms.

You can already see yourself sitting in that armchair in the corner, feeding your baby at night, tucking her back in her cot. This is going to be your space. Yours and your baby's. A little club for two.

You're starting to feel like a mum: picking out the things your baby will wear, the furniture and decor, the nappy supplies and linens. It's calming, in a way. It makes you feel like maybe you'll be okay at this; maybe you're more prepared than you thought.

And then there's packing your hospital bag. Sorting, and laying it all out on the bed. Ticking off your list and choosing your favourite pieces, folding the clothes you'll take her home in, placing them with care in your brand-new bag like you're packing to visit the Queen.

It's the ritual of anticipation. The big day is almost here.

But first, if you're lucky and your baby doesn't arrive before you're ready, you will enter the Golden Age of Maternity Leave. This is when you simply must slow down. It's your duty as a soon-to-be-mum to become a spectacularly unproductive member of society before your new job begins. Sit on the couch, watch TV, eat whatever you want, read a book, put your feet up and get ready for the chaos to begin. Never again will you have so few responsibilities. Exploit it, you lucky duck. You deserve it.

# 23

# The party to
# end all parties

Because there'll be no more parties once the baby arrives. (Jokes!)

Some people are against baby showers and I have no idea why, because:

1.  It's a party for you to get presents.
2.  Everyone will give you stuff—stuff you need and/or want.
3.  You're the centre of attention and everyone wants to celebrate you.
4.  They're going to give you stuff.
5.  You get to eat cake!
6.  Did I mention presents?

Don't feel bad about getting presents. You're actually doing people a favour because if there's one thing people love spending money on, it's baby stuff. They want to hold up the teeny-tiny socks and squeal over the littleness of them. They want to choose the most ridiculously soft onesies and itty-bitty knits. LET THEM. Don't deny your family and friends the chance to shower you and your baby with stuff. It makes people happy.

Of course, the thing no one tells you is that you don't really need 86 kilos of soft baby clothes. What you need is nappies, nappy-rash cream, baby wipes, nipple cream, baby toiletries and maybe a cleaning service for when you get home from hospital—and hopefully you have an incredible friend who has her own kids and will gift you something practical that you didn't even know you needed.

Still, clothes are cute too. Plus you'll get cake.

Embrace the party. You should be celebrated, you've done an amazing job and the biggest moment of your life is right around the corner. Kinda makes birthdays and Christmas feel like average Monday mornings in comparison.

# 24

# The only way is out

You will spend the last few weeks of pregnancy desperate to evict that child from your body. And then it will dawn on you that a baby on the inside is so much easier to take care of than a baby on the outside. Plus, getting the baby out sounds like a really unpleasant activity so you decide you simply won't give birth and you'll just keep the baby inside for at least a few more months. But . . .

## It's happening whether you like it or not

I'll say it again: it's happening, sister. One way or another, that child needs to get out of your body. And if you haven't noticed, there's no trapdoor. Something's gotta give.

Yes, your pelvis is ill-equipped for this business. It's way too small for what's going to come out. But, like Optimus Prime, you will transform, and parts of your body will shift and move to let that kid out. The baby's skull will fold over itself to let him get out of there. It's totally sci-fi.

The best thing I can say about this is that women go back for more. If it was the worst experience you could ever endure, women wouldn't do it more than once.

Also, women are bad-ass.

## The ends justify the means

By the time you're about 38 weeks pregnant, you won't care if they take to your guts with a hacksaw as long as that human being scratching at your cervix and kicking you in the lungs GETS OUT.

Mother Nature's a sneaky old cow. She makes sure you're so uncomfortable and miserable that you're begging to go into labour. And then, not long after you have that baby in your arms, she makes you forget most of what just happened.

## You can't really plan for birth

You can write a birth plan, if that makes you feel a bit more in control. But things don't often go to plan, and that can be upsetting if you'd had your heart set on a particular type of birth.

You might plan a magical water birth, with the voice of Enya floating in the air as you sniff peppermint oil for pain relief, and chant affirmations while your partner gently rubs your back.

But it's not up to you. It's up to your baby. And she might want to come out in the middle of the Coles deli section, with Rick Spring-field lusting after 'Jessie's Girl' in the background, the apprentice baker assisting, and an elderly lady fanning you with her copy of *New Idea*.

Motherhood is a complete lack of control, and it starts now.

## You might cope marvellously well

Women often find they become completely different people during the birthing process. Women who are usually calm and serene can become foul-mouthed psychopaths in labour. Women who are usually foul-mouthed psychopaths can become calm and serene.

As I laboured away, all night long, I didn't make a sound because I didn't want to wake my husband who was sleeping in the corner. Yes, I laboured in silence. Don't ask me why. I wasn't in my right mind.

## There are no awards for doing it drug free

No, *really*. There's no big prize for doing it *au naturel*. There's this belief that a woman who gives birth without drugs is better and stronger, and that resorting to pain relief denies you one of the essential rites of passage for all women and may even affect your bond with your child.

Darl, *no one cares*. Sure, women have given birth without pain relief for thousands of years, but that's only because pain relief didn't exist. You think a woman in the African desert would say no to an epidural? No chance. She'd laugh hysterically and say, GET IT IN ME, DOCTOR! Then she'd enjoy her damn self giving birth, present and lucid in the most beautiful moment of her life, because she wouldn't be out of her mind with pain.

Birth is unpredictable, uncontrollable and it's absolutely going to happen. It's a wild ride, but it's not the end of your journey. It's just the beginning.

# 25

# It's worth it

You're almost at the end of your pregnancy. You are aching and cranky and oh so exhausted. You are over it, and you want to know: is this all worth it? Other mums complain. All. The. Time. Why would anyone want to have a baby?

Today I was woken at 5.23 a.m. by a kick to the head because my five year old still comes into our bed. Every. Single. Night. It's not the snuggle-fest you might imagine. It's a nightly display of defensive martial arts because he sleeps like he's being attacked by wasps.

You know what? Still worth it.

I had a two-and-a-half-minute shower while my toddler stood and banged on the shower door because she feels deeply offended whenever my eyes aren't locked exclusively on hers. She screeched one long, continuous, ear-shattering screech while I threw on some clothes and pulled my dirty hair into a bun, telling myself I'd get around to washing it tomorrow (I won't).

It's okay. Still worth it.

I spent the whole morning arguing with my children. Please eat your breakfast, please stop pushing your sister, please put on some pants, please get off the counter, please stop karate-chopping the walls. They didn't listen to a word I said so I screamed louder and louder and louder until my throat hurt, which is nature's way of letting you know you're a terrible parent because you literally injured yourself being a bitch.

Still worth it.

This afternoon I watched the last grains of my youth fall through the hourglass as I crouched beside the toddler's cot, my back seizing up, my arm angled through the bars and numb from lack of blood, patting the bottom of a child whose chubby hands were grabbing at the top of my head, ripping out chunks of my hair in protest at being put down for a nap.

Still worth it.

My back is always aching. My eyes sting from exhaustion. Let's not even mention the dull skin, saggy tummy, ill-functioning pelvic floor . . . or the boobs. Oh my god, the boobs. My body is like a swimming costume that was once bright and stretchy but it's been through the wash one too many times and the elastic's shot, the colour has faded and the underwire has started to stick out the top. It still looks alright, but it's never going to look new again.

STILL WORTH IT.

After a dinnertime I'd rather not discuss, my toddler went galloping off down the hall like a baby deer freed from captivity. The five year old went after her and I primed myself to intervene yet again, but he didn't push her over—he jumped in front of her and yelled 'BOO!' and she dissolved into delicious little giggles. They chased each other around, squawking and whooping, and my heart filled my chest to bursting.

And that's it right there. I'd do it all again, ten times over, just for that.

I could write for days about all the joys of having children. The first smiles and giggles, the cuddles, discovering their personalities, the wonderment and pride as they learn new things, the first time they say, 'I love you'.

But my most convincing argument is that even when it's so hard you want to cry, you'll never regret it.

Today I went to the toilet with an audience of two. I hid in the pantry and ate Tim Tams just for a moment of peace. I cried when my toddler hit me with a toy car. And even in those moments, I never thought about going back to my old life. I'd still choose this life—every single time—because I've got them.

The power of the love, joy and pride coming your way is so overwhelming that you will happily endure the hardest moments of your life just for a taste of that magic.

Kids are hard. SO HARD. But we keep having them because they're SO WORTH IT.

# 26

# Your pregnancy bucket list

My friends, in the interest of really making a mark in your last few months of child-freeness, I present to you a pregnancy bucket list filled with things you really should do before this baby comes along and changes everything. They're things you might never get to do again, and you might miss them.

1.  Take a photo of your face. Really zoom in on your eyes. There may come a day when you'd like to look back at your 'before' photo.
2.  Go for a drive by yourself and turn the music up really loud. Listen to the filthiest gangsta rap you can find and shout out all the explicit lyrics.
3.  Better yet, drive in complete silence. Roll the windows up and enjoy the sound of your own breathing. Don't scream at anyone and enjoy not answering the same question 473 times.

4. Go to the toilet with the door closed. Look around at all four walls and appreciate the complete privacy of having a bowel movement alone. Really commit to memory what it feels like to not discuss your poo with another person.

5. Watch someone walk into the bathroom. Watch them leave the bathroom. Do not discuss anything they did in there.

6. Wake up when you have finished sleeping.

7. Walk into a room. Remember why you're there.

8. Read something smart. NOT RHYMING POETRY. It's imperative that it does not rhyme.

9. Make yourself a cup of tea. Make all the noise you want because no one is asleep. Drink your tea while it's still hot.

10. Leave your house on a whim. Pick up your bag and walk out the door. Don't spend an hour running through a mental check-list. Don't argue with anyone about shoes. Just get up and walk out like you are the boss of your own life.

11. Wear all your dangly earrings and enjoy your earlobes staying intact.

12. Agree to give your friend a lift and don't panic at the thought of them seeing the state of the car floor.

13. Don't talk, even if it's just for an afternoon. Enjoy not listening to your own voice. Enjoy not having to discuss the meaning of life every four minutes. Relish being able to carry out simple tasks without providing a running commentary on every muscle moved.

14. Shower every day.

15. Put a pair of scissors really close to the edge of the bench. Put a glass on the coffee table. Put a plate of food in front of someone and let them judge the temperature for themselves. Feel the adrenaline of risk-taking surge through your veins.

16. Buy yourself some clothes from a shop that doesn't have trolleys out the front.

17. Place a packet of chocolate biscuits in the middle of the room and eat the whole thing right out in the open. Do not hide in your pantry and do not share. They're all yours.

18. Have a lovely lunch with your girlfriends and appreciate how their eyes never glaze over when you're speaking.

19. Meet your partner at the end of a long day with a big kiss and a hug. Ask him about his day and listen carefully to his response with interest and empathy. Give him your undivided attention and tell him his worries will always be your top priority.

20. Cuddle your pets. Tell them again how you'll never love the baby as much as them.

21. If you are not yet pregnant, go and jump on a trampoline. Enjoy not wetting yourself.

22. Clean your home. Sit and watch it stay clean.

23. Arrive somewhere on time.

24. Watch a whole movie from beginning to end.

25. Swear frequently. Don't spell anything out. Don't use any substitutes: *sugar, shoot, fudge, far out, fa la la la la, holy moly* and *jeepers* are not to be used.

26. Eat your dinner with both hands, while it's hot.

27. Spend the hours of 4–7 p.m. thinking about yourself. Just sit and relax. Maybe take a bath. Please remember the ease of these hours. It's important.

28. Talk to someone without needing to repeat yourself 326 times before they acknowledge you are speaking.

29. Start a task. Complete it in the expected time frame.

30. Spend one final day thinking about YOU and how you might fill your day.

Now get ready for the greatest, most hectic adventure of your life.

# Part two
# Newborn days

or
*What do I do now?*

*Dear New Mumma,*

*Forrest Gump said, 'Life is like a box of chocolates, you never know what you're going to get.'*

*Oh, Forrest.*

*Mate, you're going to get a goddamn chocolate, aren't you? It's not rocket science. And if it's vitally important to know the flavour you're going to get, there's a visual guide on the inside of the box to help you out. Use your head, buddy.*

*Becoming a mother for the first time is nothing like a box of chocolates (which is ironic, given your craving for chocolate will skyrocket) unless that box of chocolates is also littered with cold hard exhaustion, self-doubt and lumps of poo. And there isn't a handy guide to let you know which is which.*

*What I'm trying to say is that if you dive into a box of chocolates, you'll probably get chocolate. Having a newborn? That's the ultimate lucky dip of life. It could be the greatest joy you've ever known, or it could send you halfway to the loony bin. And both would be completely standard.*

*Mums don't often talk about the first few weeks of motherhood, except in a vague, hazy, rose-tinted way that does nothing to prepare other mums for what's about to come.*

*In our defence, there's a legitimate reason we don't tell you about the newborn days: WE DON'T REMEMBER. Like trauma victims who can't remember the details of their injury, mothers lose the details of that first month or so.*

*Not that it's necessarily traumatic (though it can be), but the physical recovery, paired with the sleep deprivation (that you're not used to yet), mixed with the emotional uppercut you suffer as you try to wrap your mind around What The Actual Fallopian just happened . . . it's a lot for one human to process.*

*So to help us survive (and to ensure we do it all again), the brain blurs the edges a bit. It glosses over some of the yucky parts and tidies up some of those rough bits and makes the whole thing seem rather like a funny dream.*

*If we were able to remember, we'd tell you those first few weeks changed us in the most extraordinary and profound ways. You'll never be a first-time mum again. It's a pretty big deal.*

*Note: your baby is officially considered a newborn for the first four weeks, but in all honesty, it will be about twelve weeks before you come up for air and start thinking about yourself again. This is called the fourth trimester: three whole months when your baby is wishing he was still on the inside, and you're wishing you could remember what life was like before. This stage is all about surviving day to day and trying to find some sort of rhythm.*

*Good luck, lady, and remember, YOU WILL SURVIVE because you're a mum now, and it's what we do.*

*Love Lauren xx*

# 27

# Just like the movies

Movies tell us everything we need to know about giving birth.

The minute you feel a twinge in your belly, you will rush to the hospital. This will occur in a very high-stress and comedic way: you will scream very loudly (because screaming = funny), you will sweat a lot (not enough to ruin your make-up, though), your partner will mop your brow and pat your shoulder but he won't see anything going on down below, and after a few minutes a nurse will place a very clean, neatly wrapped four-month-old child on your chest.

You will instantly lose your sweaty sheen, your hair will look perfect, you will forget all the pain, and you will immediately fall in love with your flawless-looking child as all the medical staff disappear off-screen.

Yeah-nah. It doesn't work like that.

You won't go to the hospital for what feels like four days because the midwives will keep telling you not to come in even though you're pretty sure It's Bad Now. You'll drive to the hospital at the legal speed limit and make your way, slowly, on foot, to the delivery suite. When you hear the feral bellowing from an adjoining room, you'll quietly ask a nurse if perhaps it'd be best if you just went home now.

Yes, there will be screaming, but you probably won't find it funny. You might sweat but it's more likely you'll poo yourself and then turn beetroot-red from all the straining and pushing and it's possible your partner will mention at some point in the future that your pushing face isn't your prettiest. It will probably take more than a few minutes. It might even take days, and you'll probably end up in tears because it won't bloody END. The books told you that all you needed to do was walk around, rub your legs together and breathe and you'd be fine but surely something must be very wrong here because YOU'RE NOT FINE.

Your partner may be holding your hand and rubbing your shoulders but he won't miss out on the action below. When you're curled in a ball with your knees up around your ears, you'd be surprised by just how front-and-centre your vagina is. How long do you think your torso is? It's not four metres away from your face, babe. It's RIGHT THERE. One quick glance in that direction and he'll see it all.

Eventually, that baby will come out. And whether it has to be cut from your guts or yanked from your yoni, the process will most likely be savage. There's really no low-impact way for it to happen. The child they throw at you will be mucky, much tinier and a whole lot more squashed-looking than the heifers they use in the movies.

Hot tip: you aren't actually finished once the baby is out. There's still one more thing you need to deliver, and that's the placenta. There's a reason the afterbirth has never made an appearance on the silver screen. It is a sack of gore the size of your child. Don't forget to snap a happy pic with it. #afterbirth #eatitup #rawcarnage #fromyourbody #nobigdeal

I should point out, so as not to terrify the more nervous readers, that some women find the experience of childbirth spiritual, calm and empowering. Some women say it didn't hurt as much as they thought it would. Some women say they practically bounced out of the delivery suite, feeling on top of the world.

Good for them.

# 28

# 'The easy way out'

A little side note here to remind everyone that C-sections are not only legitimate but often life-or-death-vital.

Dipsticks like to scoff at caesareans being 'the easy way out' for people 'too posh to push'. Ah, what a good time those cheeky little caesars are!

Because if you bip that remote control, a little door in your belly pops open and the doctor reaches in and retrieves your baby from the top shelf in the baby aisle. Doc will snap that lid shut, and you'll be on your merry way.

No.

First, if you've had to go through the whole labour experience before being rushed to surgery, you didn't escape a thing. That's the bloody hard part, and if you add the fear and panic on top of it, you've had a really rough trot, Mumma. The magical moment of childbirth has been replaced by sterile urgency. Instead of oohs and ahhs, you've got monitors and instruments working overtime to make sure you and your baby survive. It's not a celebration of the miracle of creation—it's now a job to keep you both alive, and that can be a traumatic experience. It's not what any woman wants or plans for.

Sometimes women are given a general anaesthetic, and they miss the birth of their own child entirely. That's the opposite of easy.

But even when the C-section is scheduled because the baby is breech or it's too big or there's something physical or emotional stopping a woman from being able to give birth vaginally, it's STILL not the easy way out.

Being sliced open on a cold table while you're awake isn't the fun little procedure you might think it is. It's not a simple slice, dice and out-comes-the-baby. It's rough and physical, and the pushing and pulling will make you feel like you're about to fall right off the table as they rummage around in your insides to pull that fat little bundle out of a too-small incision. It can be scary and confronting and they'll need to take your baby away from you for a few minutes to check she's okay before wrapping her up and letting you have a 'hold'—which is more like trying to look down your nose at the little face squashed under your chin.

But it's important to know that this can be just as special and overwhelming as a vaginal birth. You don't miss out on the magic just because you're not pushing the baby out. This is still the miracle of life happening before your eyes. Giving birth is giving birth, no matter which exit the baby takes.

There is no 'easy way out'. However it happens, you're a goddamn warrior and don't let anyone tell you otherwise.

PS: Some hospitals won't let your baby stay with you while you're in recovery after a C-section. It can be a couple of hours until you're transferred to your room, which means the baby will be left with your partner or whoever has been in the theatre with you. If you think this might upset you, ask your doctor, midwife and/or hospital what their policy is and if they'll allow you to have your baby with you. Those first couple of hours can never be repeated, and the sadness over an unexpected separation can linger for years.

# 29

# Now what?

So, someone has just dumped a child on you and that child is now yours.

You are officially a mother.

Now you're a mum, you know exactly what to do to care for your child. It's instinct. It's animalistic. Some profound, long-hidden wisdom, born in your ovaries, mystically guides you, showing you how to care for this babe. You're doing exactly what you should be doing without even thinking about it.

Ha ha ha . . . jokes! That's not how it works at all.

Those instincts don't always magically appear the second you're holding your baby. There are no spontaneous lullabies; there's no invisible connection forming between you and your child. You aren't wordlessly communicating with the fruit of your loins.

You're most likely sitting there thinking, 'Oh. Okay. That happened. I have a baby. Hello there. I'm your mother. This is rather strange, isn't it?' Or maybe something with more swear words in there.

And you're waiting for instructions or permission to do something, but *no one is speaking to you.*

Medical staff don't care that this is your first time. They're busying themselves with making sure you're physically okay and they'll completely forget that delivering babies isn't your job. They've delivered 874 babies. You've delivered one. And you're sitting there, wild eyed and foggy brained, holding a hairless mammal and not sure what you should do next.

Birthing classes dish out detail after horrifying detail about the birthing process but the information stops abruptly at 'They put the baby on your chest'.

It's as if you've just arrived at your first day of a new job. It's a job you've been keen to start but you've only been given a vague outline of the tasks you'll be expected to carry out.

Everyone around you is busy at work, rushing about, clearly more experienced than you. You're sitting there, hoping someone will come along to show you to your desk, give you a computer login and a rundown of your tasks. You thought you had an idea of what you'd be doing but now you're here, you realise you're grossly underqualified for this job and it appears no one is here to supervise you.

How the hell are you supposed to get started without some sort of handover or orientation? A computer near you starts pinging and you look around, wondering if you should get up and check it out, but still, no one is talking to you. You feel like maybe that's your computer and it could be a job for you to complete, but where's the boss? Is anyone going to show you what to do?

Eventually, you'll realise your boss is The Baby—a megalomaniac sadist who gives you zero instructions or guidance and no feedback at all. He won't even email you a list of tasks. You've just got to guess what he wants you to do and if you get it wrong, he'll scream in your face until you want to cry.

It's alright, you're new to this. No one starts a new job and nails it on the first day. Or, if they nail the first day, they're going to falter a few days down the line when things become a bit more involved. But you're learning, and if you want to really grow, you've got to take leaps of faith and make mistakes. If you're not making mistakes, you're not learning anything.

So, like any first day at a new job, you're going to need to ask some questions.

Ask the medical staff if you're okay. They could be performing a vagina replacement down there and you wouldn't even know. Prompt them to communicate with you.

Ask them if the baby is okay. Even if he looks perfectly fine, it's nice to get some confirmation. Remind the staff you're new at this.

Ask them what you should be doing now, but expect anyone and everyone to give you a completely different answer because no one can agree on anything when it comes to taking care of babies. This will continue forever.

Usually, the first thing you should try to do (after taking the mandatory first photos #welcomebaby) is put your baby to your boob. But apparently, again, you're supposed to just know to do that without anyone telling you.

If no one steps up to help you, go right ahead and put that baby on your boob. You don't need to latch or actually produce anything, but putting your baby's mouth near your nipple is pretty much all your baby wants out of life so far.

Not going to lie: that first time is weird and awkward. You're putting a complete stranger's mouth on your nipple, which is not something you'd typically do in public. It's normal if it feels a bit strange and unnatural at first.

But this is *your* baby. You don't technically need to ask anyone's permission, even though you'll want to. You get to make the decisions now, and that can be the scariest realisation of all.

# 30

# Where is the love?

The moment you finally look into your baby's eyes is when you're supposed to be walloped with a love so great it leaves you breathless.

There will be fireworks, angels singing, a fairy floss machine in the corner. All good and happy things will rain down on you, instantly changing your life and awakening your soul to what it really means to be a mother. The bond will be instant and more powerful than anything in existence.

Right?

So why does this wingless pigeon feel like he could be anyone's kid? Why won't he stop squawking? Has he been in a fight? He looks like he's got two black eyes. That gunk and blood are so gross, I want to wipe it off so badly, but I don't think I'm supposed to notice that. Is everyone expecting me to kiss it? I don't want that stuff in my mouth. I really thought I'd make a better-looking kid. This one looks a bit like Nick Nolte. Why don't I think he's beautiful? Don't all mums think their babies are beautiful? Is everyone waiting for me to cry with happiness? Do I do that now or is it too late? What's the time? I wonder if it's still raining outside.

The one thing no one ever tells new mums is: when you hold your baby for the first time, you might not *feel* much at all.

If you're lying there feeling nothing more than shock and disbelief, there is *nothing wrong with you.* If you take one thing away from this book, I want it to be this.

Of course, some women do give birth and enter that dreamy, loved-up phase immediately and that's great for them. Their hormones kick in, the endorphins from labour flood their system, and it's an oxytocin party for two. Delightful.

I don't know many of those women. Most women I know are from the 'I went numb with shock and didn't know which way was up' camp.

The instant connection isn't a done deal. Feeling a lack of anything resembling love is far more common than people think but no one ever says it out loud because, well, that's just not what you do, is it?

'Introducing baby Axelotle, born this morning at 6.23 a.m., weighing 3.2 kg and measuring 51 cm. He looks a bit like a dropped pie and we're not quite sure if we like him yet.'

When your body has been through a trauma—and even if it all goes well, it's still a huge bloody trauma—your brain might prioritise your physical and mental healing over the bonding. You need a chance for your body to calm down and for your brain to process WTF just happened. But the truth is you'll have absolutely *no downtime* to recover because your job starts NOW.

So give yourself a break for not swooning over this tiny stranger just yet.

You *do* love your baby—you just don't know her yet.

Your love is a slow burn. It starts out as a fascination, a protectiveness. You stare at your creation with wonder.

It grows to affection and a primal desire to make sure the baby is okay. You start to notice how cute she is and you want to be near her all the time, even when she doesn't need you. You become accustomed to the feeling of that tiny body in your arms and you want her there as often as possible.

It could be a few days later, or it could be weeks or even months, but eventually you will look at your child and realise you are stupidly, fiercely, head-over-heels in love with this tiny person you grew. The love that has been hidden under a fog of fatigue, confusion and desperation to be a good mum has ensnared your heart so completely you can barely believe you hadn't noticed it before.

But wait, there's more!

That overwhelming love for your newborn? That's nothing. That's just the start of it.

This right here is your entry-level love. It's big, no doubt. It's HUGE. Truly bigger than anything you've felt before. Remember all that time you thought another adult was The One? Wrong. Your child is The One.

But the love is going to get bigger. And bigger. And bigger still.

That tiny infant is amazing, it's true, but let's be honest: newborns don't really *do* anything. They open their eyes, they look at you, they cry, they demand food and they poo. It's cool when it's your kid, but in retrospect you realise it's not that impressive.

Wait until your child actually starts DOING things. When your newborn turns into a baby, then a toddler, and then a child who thinks real, deep, amazing thoughts about life, your heart will swell so much that it physically hurts and you will do weird, creepy things like lie down next to their sleeping bodies so you can have a little cry into their hair . . . and other, regular unhinged stuff like that.

I don't know if there's a plateau of parental love. It's probably about the time they start telling you they hate you and want to live with their mate Spiniker because his parents let them hang out at the street races, or something. I'll let you know when I get there.

# 31

# Your vagina is having a day

Meanwhile, as you're holding this new and wrinkled stranger, there could still be quite a bit of activity happening downstairs and this could be the first time you notice just how many people are looking up your birth canal. It seems perfectly normal and necessary during labour, with one person whipping away a tray of your own faeces and another commenting on your perineum, but it seems less normal when the baby is out and you're trying to have a special moment while someone cups your crotch.

You will eventually make it to your hospital room and you'll realise you've got some healing to do.

Giving birth is rough but the bodily sacrifice doesn't end when the baby comes out.

Your poor old fanny is unhappy. She's swollen, she's sore and she's not okay with what just happened.

Ask for ice. You're going to need it. Ice is lovely down there.

Make sure the nurses are aware of your need for All The Ice. Cubes probably aren't ideal, but a nice ice block will soothe her woes. A lovely frozen condom will also do the trick. Ironic, isn't it? Using a condom down there . . . at this moment . . . right now?

Those stitches are bitches as well. Ask ALL the questions on how to care for them while you're in hospital. Write it down if you have to.

Drugs are wonderful. Don't be a hero. It's not fun to be groaning in pain every time you pick up your baby. Take as much as they'll allow you to take and remind them frequently that you need more. Cosy up to a good nurse and see how much they'll let you take home.

Take this from me: it's easier to bond with your baby when you're not in agony. If you want rosy memories of your first days and weeks as a mum, it's not going to help if you're wincing every time you move.

Then there's the blood. Technically it's called *lochia*, which means 'relating to birth'—which is cute, considering it's like a bad period that lasts for about six weeks and can drop out in chunks. When I say chunks, I mean quivering masses of tissue the size and shape of a lemon, just popping out of your vag into the shower drain like it's totally okay and you're not bleeding to death at all.

Those maternity pads are the real deal, by the way. Sure, you'll feel like you're wearing a small nappy but so is your baby, so #twinning! Keep wearing them long after the bleeding has stopped because the bleeding can restart with a vengeance. It's not enjoyable to start haemorrhaging down your bare legs in the middle of Big W when you've got a trolley full of stuff and a baby strapped to your chest. Or so I've heard.

The bleeding will still happen even if you have a caesarean, so you can't escape it, my love. No way, no how.

Let's not forget the afterbirth contractions, which are straight-up cruelty. Birth contractions give you a baby, so at least there's a reward for them. After-birth contractions happen as your uterus shrinks back down, and they can be just as strong, but the only reward is a punch to the guts.

They get worse with each child. Just so you know.

Then there's the possibility—wait, *probability*—that you'll wet yourself in the days following birth. Your poor old bladder has seen better days and your pelvic floor has a massive sinkhole right in the middle, so pissing yourself is a pretty likely outcome. No big deal, dear; if you're wearing those surfboard pads, you should be right.

Pooing yourself is also something that could happen. But some might say a spontaneous and unplanned poo is preferable to having to push it out with force. That first post-birth poo is something you'll never forget. Don't be shy about taking all the stool softeners you can get your hands on. It's best you get used to talking about poo anyway. Poo is your life now.

The hardest thing about recovering from a vaginal birth is just how crucial that whole area is.

Your minced-meat crotch is like a Jane Doe trauma victim who can't even be identified by her loved ones because the damage has left her hideously deformed and unrecognisable. But old Ground Zero still needs to get up and wee and poo and hold your organs in; she needs to be sat on, walked around with and just generally put to work immediately. It seems so unfair.

On top of this, the whole area will feel crusty and dirty. The blood, the stitches, the wee and poo and did I mention the blood? Jesus, Mary and Joseph, it's a whole lot to deal with ON TOP of the brand-new person in your life that needs to be fed and cared for. You don't even get half a day to feel sorry for yourself.

Recovery from birth can take a couple of days or it can take a couple of months. Or longer. Just because you see some mums striding along with their one week old in the pram, it doesn't mean that will be possible for everyone.

For some women, every time they stand up their reproductive organs will settle onto their pelvic floor like a bowling ball sinking through a defective hammock, threatening to fall straight through. When you've got nothing but a battered and bruised cooch, stitched together with string, holding the whole show together, it's painful. Really painful.

The poor old pet is going take some time to resemble herself. She's going to be different for a little while. My friend Kerrie called her vagina The Predator because she's a poet like that. Take it easy on yourself.

# 32

# Boob on

Being a woman is kind of bad-ass. Our bodies create people. From scratch! And when they arrive, we can provide everything they need to survive and thrive, like a self-sufficient farm. Moo. In a world of technology and science, it's a powerful feeling to know your baby only needs you.

Breastfeeding can feel like a symbol of motherhood—proof that you're a good mum, that you were meant to have this baby. That it's the two of you against the world.

But it's not as easy as just putting your baby to your boob.

## Don't let anyone tell you it shouldn't hurt

Oh, if I had a dollar for every nurse who told me 'If you're doing it right, it shouldn't hurt'. (I'd have about six dollars, but it felt like a lot at the time). I'm sorry, but unless you're a former dominatrix or you've just stepped off shift as a dairy cow, your nipples are not used to that much action. It *will* hurt.

Some women almost give up because when the pain makes their toes curl, they assume something must be wrong.

There's nothing wrong. You've just got soft little white-collar nips that have never done a hard day's work, and they've got to toughen up a bit.

## You will be milked

For the first few days of your baby's life, your boobs will basically be big ol' dummies for your baby to chew on. You might squeeze out a few drops of colostrum but no real milk.

Your milk has to 'come in'. And if you're not sure if it's 'come in' yet, IT HASN'T COME IN.

They say 'come in' like the milk will knock on a door and you'll sing out, 'Come in!' and the milk will politely open the door and there it'll be. No.

It won't be a subtle development. You won't need to be in tune with your body to know it's happened. You will wake up one morning with a couple of porn star rockmelons bolted to your chest, like someone has snuck in overnight and implanted cement under your skin. Welcome to the dairy farm, Bluebell: your milk has COME IN.

Your baby by now will be ravenous, but trying to put a wailing, furious newborn onto a concrete boulder is an exercise in futility. Poor lamb's got nothing to grab hold of. It's like trying to rock climb up a window.

So your boobs feel like they might actually split open, your baby is livid and thrashing at your skin, and in waltzes a nurse . . . to *milk you*. You heard me.

Have you ever been milked before? No? Well, let me assure you that having a stranger grab your boob and *squeeze your teats* will make you reassess everything you've ever known about yourself. Again, medical staff can forget this is all new for you, so they'll swan on in, grab your rock-hard breast without a word and get to milking. Yes, just like a cow.

Another fun technique nurses love is the old 'bub-smash'. This can happen when your baby is squealing like a stuck pig and you are mentally packing your bags and preparing your getaway, and a midwife barges in, grabs your child's head in one hand and your over-inflated goon bag in the other and smacks them together, as if the surprise attack will shock you both into just bloody getting it right.

Where did they even come up with this? Back in the olden days, when a little villager woman had just given birth and her baby was struggling to latch, did she just belt her kid in the face with her tit in frustration and then, to her surprise, find that he opened his mouth and started suckling? Did she then spread the word among the womenfolk about this new trick where you sock the kid as hard as you can with your boob?

## This is your full-time job now

Adults eat three times a day. Or if you're a grazer like me, about five. Either way, adults spend a civilised percentage of their day on food.

Newborns eat eight to twelve times a day.

I'll wait while you do the maths.

YES, that's every TWO TO THREE HOURS, 24 hours a day. Yes, even in the middle of the night. The only thing you do now is feed the baby. Better pull up a comfy chair; you're going to be in it forever.

I should point out: that's not a two-hour break in between feeds; that's two hours from the beginning of one feed until the beginning of the next. If you start at 9 a.m., you're going to need to start the next one at 11 a.m. A slow eater can take up to an hour to feed so that leaves you a one-hour break in between feeds. One hour to stand up, go to the toilet, eat something and sit back down to start all over again. This titbit of info never seems to be mentioned to a mother-to-be because WHO would sign up for that?

But eight to twelve times a day is nothing if you've been through a cluster feed. 'What's a cluster feed?' you ask. Oh, a cluster feed is when your baby is going through a growth spurt and decides to eat non-stop, so you sit, trapped under your child, feeding every half hour until you're not sure if you're a human or a tree anymore and you can't spell your name and you've forgotten how to speak.

Your baby doesn't care that you're exhausted, bleeding, in pain and possibly vomiting from the pain relief you're on (yep, that can happen). The baby must be fed. Your needs are inconsequential.

This is how babies break us. I'm sure it's in *The Art of War* some-where, where you crush the spirit of your captives so they lose their sense of self and submit fully to your control. So if you survive a couple of days of cluster feeding (and it does end, I promise), your transformation from independent woman to baby slave is complete. Well done.

## The let-down can be fierce

Hot pins and needles. A vice tightening on your mammaries. Straight-up fire. As the milk lets down (starts to flow) it can cause an intense sensation—sometimes painful, sometimes uncomfortable, sometimes strangely mixed with a giddy dose of oxytocin. You'll feel a raging Saharan thirst and after skolling a litre of water, you'll need approximately half a packet of biscuits to chase it down with.

The milk doesn't come out of just one hole, by the way. That nipple is like a nifty little fountain, spraying milk out all sides. Some babies will be lucky enough to get a mother whose let-down is like a steady, reliable garden sprinkler. Other babies will get a mother who moonlights as a human water cannon with the riot police, keeping the great unwashed under control with her mammaries.

These are often the mums whose milk lets down any old time of day or night—at the supermarket check-out, at dinner with the in-laws, signing for a package with the postman. No baby necessary, just 'Hello! I'm leaking!'.

A shower is always a fun time for a new mother, the warm water setting off a symphony of leaks. Boobs spraying the walls, wee and lochia running down the drain. Hot, bitter tears of exhaustion joining the chorus. Ah, motherhood.

But if you're able to get the whole thing working, when you've pushed through the initial pain and accepted your fate as a couch-dwelling, boobs-out dairy cow—this could be the most beautiful part of becoming a mother for you. Truly.

Being able to feed your child whenever, wherever, with the food you make yourself is precious. It's easy, it's portable, it's always the right temperature, it's free! It's the perfect way to settle a hungry child, a tired child, a scared or upset child. It's a cure-all for babies. Whatever it is, try the boob first and watch the spell being cast.

You look down at sleepy lashes, chubby fingers on your chest, pink cheeks filled with sweetness and realise you are the life-source for your greatest achievement. It's intoxicating.

Unless it's not.

# 33

# Boob off

The 'natural', instinctual ritual of breastfeeding doesn't always work. Enduring the struggle—or accepting the 'failure'—can almost break some women.

It might be 'natural', it might be what our bodies are 'supposed to do', but for some women it'll be the hardest thing they've ever done.

It'll be the pain for some—a pain so bad it makes them nauseous. No matter what they do—using nipple shields, checking for tongue ties, going to countless appointments with lactation consultants—some women will never be able to feed without pain. Cracked and bleeding nipples that never get a chance to heal, thrush, mastitis . . . putting a hungry baby onto the breast can feel like sticking a rusty knife into a bullet wound. Over and over and over again.

The fear of the next feed can leave you dreading being near your baby. If you need to spend hours and hours a day feeding, it's hours and hours in pain.

For others it'll be a lack of milk supply. Some women will torture themselves, trying to make more milk—all the drugs, herbal supplements and round-the-clock pumping to FORCE their bodies to produce more. For some, it won't matter what you do: that milk won't come, and the screaming, hungry baby will tear at your heart like nothing you've ever felt before.

We need to feed our babies. It's our number one instinct. It's survival. Eating means living, and not being able to feed your baby because your body just won't let you is a crushing blow. Even though logically we know switching to formula is the best plan for everyone—for the baby's survival and for our own mental health—it can still cause grief that lingers long after the baby has weaned.

The thing no one tells you is: sometimes it's your baby's fault. You could be doing everything right—you could have milk for days and be raring to go—but some little possums can never quite figure it out. A tongue or lip tie, a recessed chin, plain old fussiness ... some little tackers just can't do it and you'll both end up in pain and tears because of it.

Some women will have to work at it. They'll work so hard, for months and months on end, to feed their babies. They'll push through the pain, they'll turn their lives upside down to get their supply going, they'll exclusively pump for babies who simply can't get their latch happening.

The determination and dedication of some mothers to feed their babies is mind blowing. Even when their bodies are telling them to stop, they push through because it's important to them.

But sometimes strength comes in seeing that a happy mum and a fed baby are more important than any expectation you may have placed on yourself.

Sometimes, strength means letting go.

# 34

# The birth of a mother

On that first night, when the hospital falls quiet and you're sitting in your bed, staring at this hours-old person you made, it's hard to absorb exactly what's happened to you.

Let me tell you.

Your child was born. And so were you.

You became a mum.

Yes, *you*.

It's so weird, isn't it? People keep calling you 'Mum' and you're like, 'But Mum is a woman called Penny who still calls me to remind me to send birthday cards to people and sends me articles like "Why Bottled Water Is Bad For You" . . . so I can't be "Mum", can I?'

Yep, you can.

The title Mother is given instantly. The baby is handed to you, and hello—you are a Mother.

But the transition to 'Mum' takes a little longer.

At first it's like an ill-fitting bra, digging and pulling and throwing your posture off. You can't get comfortable because it just doesn't feel quite right.

Bit by bit, the straps loosen, the wire dislodges from your ribs, and one day—without even noticing it happen—you realise you're comfortable.

A child's journey into adulthood is called adolescence. A woman's journey into motherhood is called *matrescence*. It's a similarly significant, life-altering evolution into a new stage of being, but most people have never heard of it.

When a baby is born, we celebrate the baby. This little life, so new to the world, is loved and cherished by all.

But we don't celebrate the other birth—the birth of the mother. We don't gather around and hold that woman in our arms and let her know how special she is and how loved she'll be through this journey. We don't comfort and calm her. We don't even speak to her about this massive change in her life. We just carry on like nothing has happened, and expect her to do the same.

But something has happened. Something huge. Something magnificent. Something confusing and isolating—which is bizarre, given it's so common. Every day, more and more women enter their matrescence and yet most people don't even know this metamorphosis has a name.

Why should it be so isolating? Why do we ignore it and let her battle through it alone? Why don't we, at the very least, acknowledge that she's changing?

Wouldn't things feel much more normal, much more manageable, if we could name it? If we could say to people, 'Please excuse me, I'm just going through my matrescence right now.' And people would say, 'Oh, of course, we totally understand.'

Some particularly mature kids will travel through adolescence without an issue; in the same way, some particularly maternal women slip from womanhood into motherhood without pause. One day they're not mums, the next day they are—and off they go, into the sunset with their bedazzled MUM jackets slung over their shoulders, never even looking back at who they were before.

Some women sit in the storm of change for months, riding the wave of hormones and physical changes, fighting the Before and After and never quite grasping the Now with both hands.

Some women struggle to reconcile the mother they *thought* they'd be with the mother they are. Some feel betrayed by how little they'd been told about this process of change. Some feel confused and unprepared because it is *nothing* like the stories they'd been told. Some feel the pull of their old life, and the guilt over not being more present with their child can drag them under. These women aren't depressed or broken, they're just having a harder matrescence than some.

There's an emotional tug-of-war we don't explain to new mothers. We don't tell them it's okay to not always love motherhood—even though they love their baby. We don't give them permission to feel unfulfilled. We don't give them space to assemble all the new parts of their soul before we expect them to be settled and happy in this new skin.

And so they feel lonely, isolated, confused and overlooked. They don't understand what's happening to them and they don't feel like they can talk about this huge upheaval because they're supposed to be happy, right? They're supposed to be in love and fulfilled and devoted to their child. But this almost never happens straight away.

We give teenagers time to travel through their adolescence. And, with time, they overcome the bad skin, the foul moods, the inability to string a sentence together. Their bodies change, their emotions realign and their brains completely rewire themselves. They move into adulthood with support and understanding.

Mothers need this too. A mother's body changes, her emotions realign, her brain completely rewires itself. Mothers need time to learn who they are again, to settle in to this new version of themselves, to let their hormones adjust and their bodies heal. And, eventually, when they've been given the support and understanding they need, they'll move into motherhood with ease.

# 35

# What even is motherhood?

Stories of motherhood usually follow one of two plots: a tale of overwhelming love and joy, or a saga of toil and sacrifice.

The tales of love and joy are fairy tales. They're romanticised versions of reality featuring a sensibly dressed, brain-dead robot woman who smiles benignly while her child paints masterpieces in his sweet sailor outfit #blessed.

The sagas of toil and sacrifice are horror stories designed to glorify the wretched, starring a woman so spent she can't even drag on pants in the morning as she battles with her filthy, screaming children who've stolen her will to live.

Both of these stories are fiction.

Motherhood is so much more complicated and nuanced than any trite or cautionary tale. Motherhood involves every emotion in the book. It's a revolving door of good and bad and crazy and wonderful and hideous and fulfilling and mundane.

A mother can never be just one thing. A mother is everything, all at once.

It's the knowledge that you can't go back. This is a forever kind of job.

It's discovering there's no break. It's relentless and you never could have known how exhausting it would be.

It's learning you can do it. Even when you're shattered and emotional, you can still show up and perform. Even when you think you'll break, you keep going. Who knew you had so much strength?

It's suddenly understanding how remarkable women are. Look at what we do! We create people and then we give every last drop of ourselves to keep them alive and happy. It's the most selfless, astonishing and bad-ass thing you've ever seen and it feels wrong that everyone's carrying on like it's no big deal. Where are all the street parties and gold medals for mums?

It's wanting to give every single part of yourself to your baby, but learning that's impossible. Taking care of yourself is essential but you'll struggle to find the balance every day from now.

It's finding out that your happiness is directly linked to another person. When she is happy, you are happy. When she's upset, you are upset. Your heart is in her hands.

It's coming to terms with the mania in your head as you become this new version of yourself. You'll feel conflicted every damn day. So confident and yet so unsure. So exhausted but so motivated. So in love, and so defeated. So empowered and so unseen. So lonely but never alone.

Your story is one of adventure, and the hero is you. You start out as you—the old you. You have a baby, you lose yourself, you find yourself again, you change and evolve, you learn and you grow, you face each challenge head-on because there is no other way around it. You will find things in yourself you never even imagined were there—more patience, more understanding, more empathy than you thought possible. You will see the world and all its flaws with fresh eyes.

One day you'll look at this tiny creature and think, 'How did I ever survive without you? What did I ever do before you were here?' because everything is now framed by your love for your child.

You're a mum now. You're part of this great tradition of women, centuries of goddesses who create life and devote their being to raising their children. Every step you take has been walked before you. You're part of it now. The Motherhood.

Welcome.

# 36

# Move aside please

So now that I've told you all of that, it might come as a bit of a shock when you realise no one is coming to visit YOU.

As the crowds start to arrive, you'll finally realise something that's been niggling at you since you gave birth. Something shifted in those minutes after the baby arrived but you haven't been able to put your finger on it until now.

It seems you have become INVISIBLE.

It can be quite a shock when you first realise it. You've gone from being a pregnant goddess, fussed and fawned over like a precious baby deer. People were genuinely concerned about your health and welfare. You were the most important person in every room you walked into and you kinda liked it. I do hope you enjoyed that.

What you didn't realise is that as soon as that little person separated from your body, people stopped caring about you.

You are no longer the most important person in the room; that is now The Baby. You are no longer 'Jennifer'; you are: 'Isabelle's mum'.

Your visitors don't want to see you, I'm sorry to say. They want to see The Baby. They don't want to hear about you, they want to hear about The Baby. You will feel wildly popular and invisible all at the same time as people travel from far and wide to visit you-but-not-actually-you, just The Baby.

This lingers long after you leave hospital, by the way. If you visit someone and you don't bring The Baby, the fallen smiles and quiet sighs will cut you like a knife. They'll try to hide it but you'll know.

The Grandparents won't try and hide it at all. They'll be openly hostile about the fact you've dared to arrive without their grand-child. They'll sit and stare at you like a plug of green snot hanging from a toddler's nose, wishing they could just grab a tissue and wipe you away.

For your own sake, I suggest you never be in their presence without your child. If you accidentally bump into them without The Baby, you'll probably need to let them babysit to make up for it even though it wasn't your fault. Actually, just let them have as much contact with your child as possible to safeguard against the resentment that could build when they don't get enough time with their precious baby. And yes, I mean Their Baby. You didn't think this was just your baby did you? Oh, pet.

# 37

# Hospital life for the win

You'll hear a lot of women talk about wanting to leave hospital as soon as they can so they can get home where they're comfortable. It's all, 'Can't wait to get home!' and 'Just wanna get out of here!' and 'Comforts of home!' etc.

Those women are missing the whole point of being in hospital. HOSPITAL IS AWESOME.

- You are fed. Okay, so the food might not be the best, but you didn't have to make it and that's the most important thing. And if the food is truly terrible, you just send someone out to get you takeaway. You're allowed to eat whatever you like now, so PARTY ON, GIRLFRIEND. Make sure any visitors bring you food. Cakes, biscuits and slices are ideal for the ravenous breastfeeding mother.

- You have all the help you need. Having midwives on tap is the ultimate safety net in those first few days. If you get a few good ones, they'll hold your hand, pat your back, lend their shoulder and give you a good talking to when you need to step up and take charge. A good midwife will make you feel like you and your baby might just survive.

    Of course, they're not all good. Some midwives have the ability to make you feel small, dumb, ill-equipped and unfit with just a sigh and a roll of their eyes. These midwives think new mothers are a stain on society and can't quite comprehend how anyone can be this DUMB because you asked if you should bath the baby yet. Just know that these midwives are wrong. You aren't dumb, you're just unlucky to be lumped with a nurse who hates her job. Forget these ones and cling onto the lovely ones.

- You don't have to get out of bed. This is the most important part. When you go home and people come to visit you, it's customary to be sitting up, dressed and somewhat presentable. This is a pain in the stitches.

- In hospital there are visiting hours. Once you're home, there's no security to call, so if you have an inkling someone's going to be a squatter, tell them to see you at the hospital. Because— listen to me—YOU DON'T WANT THEM AT YOUR PLACE.

    When people come to your home, you need to get up and make pleasant conversation. Your home needs to be relatively sanitary (you know you won't be okay with people seeing how you really live). You need to provide some sort of refreshment. And they can stay as long as they want. So hear me when I say you want them to *come to the hospital.*

    At hospital, they have the choice of sitting on the end of the bed, standing beside the bed or fighting over the solitary plastic chair. There are people coming in and out all the time so there's no privacy. There are strict visiting hours that must be obeyed, and if they're not, a quick, knowing nod to a passing nurse will result in them being escorted out of your room. This means their visit will be short and sweet.

And you don't even need to move from your perch on the bed. You can sit there like royalty while everyone else swarms around you. Don't underestimate how lovely it will be to just sit, with zero obligation to entertain. You can be in your pyjamas with no make-up and dirty hair and this is perfectly acceptable, if not expected.

You might not be in your cosy bed, with all your creature comforts, but being in hospital is infinitely less work than going home. Milk it for all it's worth before you're forced out of the plane to crash-land in reality.

# 38

# Going home (or WTF?)

They literally hand you a baby, and say goodbye.

You walk out the doors of the hospital, looking back over your shoulder, waiting for someone to come and show you how to do it all. But they don't.

You walk to your car, put your baby in her seat, take another look back at the hospital and wait for someone to stop you. But they don't.

You climb into the passenger seat and then change your mind and get into the back of the car because you can't just leave the baby sitting back there all by herself, can you? Your partner starts the car and you stare desperately out the window as your car crawls away. SURELY someone is going to stop you now. But they don't.

Your partner drives at 12 kilometres an hour all the way home. You walk through your front door with your baby and stand in the middle of your home wondering if ANYONE is going to pop their head in to let you know what to do now. But they don't.

They just LET YOU TAKE THE BABY HOME.

She's yours now. No one is coming to take her away and no one will be watching to make sure you're doing it right. ALL the decisions are yours and you've simply got to figure it out on your own. It's terrifying.

Don't they know you've never done this before? This isn't putting together a tricky jigsaw puzzle, or riding a bicycle. This is a whole living human being and the stakes seem ridiculously high. And yet no one seems to care.

The weight of responsibility rendered me stupid. Standing in my lounge room, holding my baby, staring at my husband, I couldn't think of a single thing to do. I couldn't for the life of me think of what I'd normally do if I'd just walked into my own home. I couldn't even try to come up with something by myself. We had to have a discussion about whether we should just sit on the couch and hold the baby for a bit. We eventually turned on the TV even though that felt way too normal considering we now had an extra human living with us. Like, maybe we should have done a tour of our home and brought out the fancy china to impress him? I didn't want our new housemate to think we were lazy slobs who just did boring things like watch TV. We eventually accepted that sitting and watching TV would be how we'd exist for the next few weeks at least. But, good lord, it felt strange.

Going home can bring with it all sorts of expectations about what you'll be doing each day. Social media is *not* the place to go for tips on how to spend your day.

'Going for a jog on the beach with the peanut!'

'Just baking some healthy breastfeeding muffins!'

'Popping out for some brunch with the bebe #blessed!'

Nope.

Some new mums will take to social media to prove they're coping. They need the world to watch them, trotting around with their infant, filled with joy and gratitude.

Some mums simply can't do it. But there aren't a lot of posts on Facebook saying, 'Sat for fifteen hours straight. Only stood up to wee and grab a fresh tub of Nutella. But I did watch two seasons of *Game of Thrones*, so it wasn't a complete write-off'.

If you feel like going for a hike with your infant strapped to your back wearing miniature Kathmandu and soft-soled Salomons, you go get it, you sprightly little minx.

But if you want to sit on your arse in your trackie daks, that's okay too.

Sloth time is limited with babies. Your ability to sit and do nothing will come to an end pretty soon, so don't rush it. And remember that the vast majority of new mums are doing the same. It's just not very Instagrammable.

# 39

# The bubble

This is your time to exist in The Newborn Bubble. It's the happy little place new mums and dads enter when they have a newborn. It's a dreamy little land, built for bonding, healing and chocolate, where exhausted parents stare at their delectable child for hours and hours and hours at a time. They'll sit down for morning tea, stare at their baby, and nekminit it's 4 p.m., no one has showered and the cat is yowling for food and/or attention.

The Bubble is a lovely place. Don't rush out of it. Some clever parents will hole up and stay in The Bubble for months, only surfacing to post multiple pictures on social media before popping back for a little more staring, toe kissing and head sniffing.

The world can wait. It'll be exactly the same when you re-enter it; you're not missing a thing. Promise.

# 40

# The darkest days

The 'Baby Blues' is a whimsical little name for what is essentially a switch in your brain that makes EVERYTHING devastating. The sight of your partner's face, the theme music to *Home and Away*, the apple muffin the hospital gave you for morning tea. SO MANY TEARS.

Up to 80 per cent of women will go through a dark period that hits about three or four days after giving birth. You'll be teary, overwhelmed, anxious, moody and fed up. Your hormones are trying to sort themselves out but some of them are way off track, wandering aimlessly in the bush, no clue how to make it back to camp. You're kind of a mess, inside and out.

So, is it any surprise that a lot of women feel a distinct lack of wonder, love and awe in those first few days with their child? Is it any wonder that so many women lose their minds completely on the third day, as they're driving home with this tiny mystery strapped into their car? Is it so surprising that a lot of women feel overwhelmed and numb instead of dreamy eyed and ecstatic?

Everyone deals with this monumental change of life differently. Some people will keep going like nothing has changed, some will find the challenge exhilarating, and some will barely scrape by. Some will be dragged into a deep spiral of anxiety or depression.

The 'Baby Blues' should only last about three days and you'll pull through unscathed, especially if you have a supportive partner or family around you.

But sometimes the blues linger. Sometimes—no matter how supportive your partner is and how cute your baby is—you just can't force yourself to feel like *you*.

It can happen immediately or it can tap you on the shoulder, months and months down the line.

It can hit you suddenly or it can grow slowly and steadily until it almost drowns you.

It can happen to the strong, the brave, the educated, the intelligent, the popular, the terminally happy, the experienced mums and the new.

It can happen because of the sudden drop in hormones after giving birth, it can happen because of the sheer physical toll of what your body has just been through. It can hit after a traumatic birth experience. It can be the sudden and overwhelming change to your life, your relationship and your freedom. It can be brought on by the devastating effects of severe sleep deprivation. It can be a combination of all these things.

You might be teary, you might not want to eat or you might want to eat everything. You might be consumed with anxiety or you might feel nothing at all. You might struggle to fall asleep even though you're exhausted. You might want to stay at home all the time, not because you're tired and can't be bothered to get out of your comfy pants, but because you just don't want to do anything or see anyone. You might have no interest in anything. You might start to feel detached from everyone and everything including your baby. You might even start to resent the baby and the impact he's had on your life.

A new mum's mental health can be attacked from so many angles it's hard to define in just a few words.

So many mums will feel some of these things at one point or another. It's easy to write it off as normal 'new mum stuff'. *All* new mums are tired, they *all* feel exhausted and anxious. They all have moments where they feel annoyed at their baby and their partner.

But if you feel like maybe this is a bit more—like you can't see the light at the end of the tunnel—now is the time to go and chat to your doctor because YOU DON'T HAVE TO FEEL LIKE THIS.

In Australia, 1 in 10 mums and 1 in 20 dads struggle with anxiety or depression during pregnancy. This rises to 1 in 7 mums and 1 in 10 dads after birth. So many parents suffer in silence because they feel guilty they're not coping better. They feel shame that they're not enjoying parenthood more. They feel fear about not bonding with their baby.

Sometimes speaking up seems like a step too big to take, as if saying the words out loud will tip you over the edge. But if you're despairing about the future and wondering if you'll ever be happy again, it's time to fix that.

If you had a sore throat, you'd go to the doctor. If you had an infection, you'd take antibiotics. Postnatal depression and anxiety are medical problems that can be fixed.

You can speak to a GP, or a maternal health nurse. Go and let someone know that something feels off and let them help you make it better. You're a mum now and taking care of yourself is as important as taking care of your baby. YOU are important. Nobody survives if you're not okay.

And you will be okay. With some time, some counselling, some self-care and maybe some medication, you will get through this. And your bond with your baby will be stronger than ever. This time of darkness won't affect the love you and your child will have for each other.

The national organisation for perinatal anxiety and depression in Australia is PANDA. They have support resources for women and men experiencing depression and anxiety during pregnancy and after birth. Their number is 1300 726 306.

Or you can call Lifeline on 13 11 14.

You don't have to do this alone. There are so many people who want to help you.

*Hey, new mum,*

*How're you going? Has anyone asked today?*

*I mean, your fanny probably feels like it's been kicked by a donkey— or your guts feel like they've been hacked open with a rusty blade so looters could rummage inside. So take it easy on yourself, okay?*

*But what about emotionally? Are you coping? It's okay if you're not. Hell, your body has just been turned inside out and you've been lumped with a tiny human and waved on your merry way. (Like, who thought that was a good idea?) It just feels irresponsible. And IRREVERSIBLE. You absolutely cannot change your mind now.*

*But you're in love. And you're scared. And you're so very, very tired it makes you want to cry. It's no wonder you feel a bit like you're losing your mind.*

*Babe, for these first few weeks you'll be in survival mode. Your survival. Your baby's survival. You're still trying to decide if you'll let your partner survive because he's pretty useful with the baby but, screw me sideways, when it's 2 a.m. and he's snoring like a bachelor on an island cruise, you want to put a pillow over his peaceful frigging face and be done with it.*

*So yeah, emotions are running high right now. It can all feel like way too much.*

*Darling, it gets better.*

*I'll be honest: the first six to twelve weeks are rough. You'll be tired like you never knew what tired was before. You'll be scared and anxious and angry and overjoyed. You'll feel like you've dropped out of society completely.*

*So I'm asking: how are you? YOU.*

*If you're worried you're not really supposed to feel like this, tell someone. It's not permanent. It'll pass: as long as you talk to someone.*

*It gets better. I promise.*

# 41

# Wake up sleepyhead

Fresh, new babies are delicious. Those tiny curled-up koalas spend the first week or two snoozing the day away, letting out precious little squeaks and pips, and acting for all the world like a low-maintenance pet. So much for all the terrible stories of havoc and chaos!

These freshies make their parents believe they got a 'good baby', the legendary, mythical creature spoken about by old ladies in the supermarket.

'Is he a *good* baby?' they'll ask. Oh yes, he's *very* good. He's quite charitable, volunteers at the homeless shelter, has never touched a drop of alcohol. All round, we're terribly proud.

These babies cause brand-new parents to say awful, rotten, embarrassing things like: 'She's a really calm baby, because *we* are really calm. She just goes with the flow because we don't spoil or fuss over her. Babies pick up on stress, you know? And gosh, she loves her sleep! I even had to ask the midwife if I should wake her up for a feed! LOL.'

Truth is, being born is quite an ordeal. You're swimming around in your temperature-controlled spa bath, with the white noise, and in-built rocking system. And then you're ejected into a cold, bright alternate universe, populated by giants who grab at you and yell all day long. It's enough to make you want to close your eyes and pretend it never happened.

Of course, some kids are less traumatised. They're nosy little divas who come out with their eyes wide open, needing to know WHO has done this and WHY, and they're going to face the world head-on, with an unnerving stare and combat in their eyes that says, 'I'm HERE, dear.'

Most kids, however, will have a good long sleep, waking only to feed and poo. Actually, they're pretty happy to poo in their sleep as well. It's impressive to see what a child can push out without so much as a flick of the eyelid.

But then they wake up.

They send their once-cocky parents insane with their total refusal to just Go To Sleep. Mum is Googling to see if all the Nutella she's been eating this week has come through her breastmilk and she's writing a new shopping list because clearly she needs to quit all sugar and every-thing with any trace of caffeine or flavour. Meanwhile Dad's walking laps of the house trying to get the baby to close her eyes and wonder-ing if they need to go to the doctor because he's pretty sure the baby is tired but when they put her down she just won't go to sleep. WHY DOESN'T SHE SLEEP? She's tired! SLEEP IS AMAZING, CHILD. TRY IT! Mum is screaming from the next room, 'Make sure you put her down DROWSY BUT AWAKE or she'll never SELF-SETTLE!' and Dad's trying to figure out how drowsy is drowsy but still awake.

They do a happy dance when the baby finally drops off and feel like they've finally figured it out until the baby opens her eyes again, fifteen minutes later. Because apparently falling asleep is easy but staying asleep is impossible. WHAT IS WRONG WITH HER?

But there's nothing wrong with the baby. She just woke up. When she'll go back to sleep is anyone's guess. Could be a few weeks. Could be years. Who knows?

You have just entered the shadowy realm of The Great Sleep Conspiracy.

Babies don't sleep just because you put them down. I need you to know this because The Great Sleep Conspiracy would have you believe that newborns can be 'trained' to sleep 'through the night' after just a couple of weeks.

Most parents will, at some point, fall down the rabbit hole of sleep advice and once you're down there, you may never come out. Everything you read will convince you that you are setting your child up for failure. The rocking is wrong. The cuddling is wrong. The feeding to sleep is wrong. Touching is wrong. Even looking your child in the eyes is wrong because it's 'stimulating', which is really, *really* wrong. You might as well let them snort a line of coke for all that stimulation you're throwing at them.

Meanwhile, all you want to do is hold your baby. Your body wants it, your heart wants it, but your brain is telling you, 'No! The baby will never sleep if you set him up with bad sleep habits!'

You will lose your mother-loving mind if you keep trying to ignore your instincts. Your whole body will ache with wanting to pick up and soothe your baby when he needs it. It will feel so idiotic to wake your baby who has fallen asleep while feeding, just so you can put him down to sleep again. Why would you do that? Because someone on the internet told you to? Because some woman in your mother's group gave you side-eye when you said you feed your baby to sleep? Because Great Aunt Barbara told you babies will be spoilt if you hold them all the time?

We need to stop driving new mums insane with all the sleep advice. We need to support mums to do whatever helps them get through the days. If everyone's getting some sleep, celebrate that. It is not a problem unless it's a problem for *you*.

Trying to force your child to sleep will make you miserable. You might eventually succeed, but at what cost? And for how long? Infants have a stinking reputation for consistency. What they do this week flies out the window next week.

So here's the real story about baby sleep: it's really common for babies to not sleep through the night until at least six months of age. Some won't get near a whole night of sleep until well past their first birthday.

- This does not make them a 'bad baby'. Bad babies are babies who hold up bottle shops and torture kittens. If your baby doesn't do these things, you have a 'good baby' who sleeps like a 'normal baby'.
- This does not make you a 'bad mother'. You haven't failed anything. You aren't an idiot. You haven't missed something obvious. There isn't an easy trick that you just haven't read about yet. You are normal and your baby is normal. All the people talking about sleep routines for three-week-old babies are NOT NORMAL.
- The Sleeping Baby is not a badge of honour. It's not a symbol of success. It's not a sign that you're a natural. If your baby doesn't like sleep, he doesn't like sleep. If he does like sleep, he likes sleep. Your role in this is minimal.

Some babies sleep. Some babies don't. Some babies will sleep for a good six-hour stretch at night but can't go for more than fourteen minutes during the day. Some babies will do a solid three-hour kip during the day but will wail all night. (Catnapping babies are just as torturous as the night owls.)

You could work your arse off, 'training' your baby to sleep through the night by the age of three months, but then the four-month sleep regression comes along and you're back to square one, because BABIES DON'T SLEEP. And if they do sleep now, they won't sleep next month and if they aren't sleeping now, they'll probably start next month. They change constantly and you could pull your hair out trying to force it, or you can get through it one day at a time and trust that, eventually, they'll figure it out.

So hold your baby if you want. Cuddle him all day long. Feed him to sleep, rock him, pat him, do whatever makes you happy because, honestly, cuddling your baby to sleep is one of the greatest joys of motherhood. What's more precious than a sleeping baby in your arms—a baby who feels safe, loved, protected? Nothing at all. Stop feeling guilty about it. Enjoy it.

# 42

# So this is what tired feels like

The trap here is that we use the word 'tired'. Everyone knows what 'tired' feels like. It makes you feel a bit unmotivated and lazy and like you can't wait to fall into bed.

But parents aren't 'tired'. Parents *wish* they were tired. What parents feel is a whole different word that doesn't actually exist.

Parents are one closed eye away from sleep at all times. But they're not lying down in bed; they're walking through the shops, strapping their babies into car seats, trying to hold conversations, all while their bodies are tutting and sighing, putting up the 'closed' sign and tapping their feet waiting for home time.

What do you call it when your eyelids feel like sandpaper, grinding off the outer layers of your eyeballs? Or when your brain is just cottonwool pulsing inside your forehead? When people ask if you're okay and all you hear is 'apple fairy ottoman' and you can taste the couch in your mouth and walking feels dangerous?

Exhausted? Weary? Drained? Nope, none of them sound quite right.

You're a husk. A shell. A barely animated corpse, incapable of processing how tired you are but pretty sure you're on the brink of death.

What do you expect when you've had a total of 42 minutes of broken sleep in four weeks?

Because 'sleep like a baby' doesn't mean what you think it does.

Somewhere along the line, people have become confused and believe that to 'sleep like a baby' means 'to sleep soundly and contentedly'. But anyone who's ever had a baby will know this is *not* a thing.

Babies sleep fitfully, sometimes in bursts as short as ten minutes at a time, and they sound like they're being choked while they do it.

Babies are the loudest sleepers, which makes it really bloody annoying when they're in a bassinet next to your bed all night and you'd really like to go to sleep but your body is now in mum-mode, which means you wake up at the slightest sound, ever-alert for feeds and emergencies.

So while your baby snorkels away next to you, you lie awake and try to find it cute but instead just silently rage at your partner who seemingly doesn't worry about emergencies in the middle of the night because he is the one sleeping 'like a baby'. Actually, he's 'sleeping like a father'.

New mums tally up their minutes of sleep with the accuracy of a government tax auditor. Every minute gained and lost will be accounted for. And in that mental spreadsheet there's a hidden column tallying up the minutes of sleep their partner is getting. It never balances out.

The bone-aching exhaustion affects every part of your life. It can make you angry, weepy, moody and spiteful. People getting more sleep than you are sitting ducks. The mere suggestion that someone else might be tired will send a new mum into a mind-melting rage.

'*YOU* are tired? YOU DON'T KNOW WHAT TIRED IS, MOFO. I slept for fourteen minutes last night. I fell asleep on the toilet this morning. I WALKED STRAIGHT INTO A WALL AND I DIDN'T EVEN CARE BECAUSE I GOT TO CLOSE MY EYES FOR A FEW SECONDS. Tell me again how tired you are.'

New parents spend a lot of time trying to spot the baby's tired signs. This is a set of jerky movements, ear-pulls and hieroglyphs that let you know they need to be put down for a nap. Spoiler alert: if they're awake, they're tired. Put them to bed.

But everyone is so focused on how much sleep the baby is getting no one notices that mum is standing there wearing gumboots and a shower cap, brushing her teeth with a candle and obsessively staring at her jerking infant and trying to decide if he's tired or trying to communicate through modern dance.

Here's a guide to a mother's tired signs that your loved ones might find useful. Feel free to distribute.

## Yawning

If you spot a mother stifling a yawn, it's likely she's had a night of broken sleep. She's going to need plenty of caffeine to survive the day. Hand that mum a coffee.

Note: it's safe to assume that every mother with a baby is this tired as a default. If she is not this tired, she has a unicorn baby. Or she's on the good drugs. Either way, good on her.

## Fake smile

If you are trying to talk to a mother and she is giving you the wide-eyed fake smile, it's likely she is very tired. She thinks if she opens her eyes really wide she might trick herself into feeling awake.

Please don't be offended if you need to repeat yourself eight times before she responds with a noncommittal 'Mmmm'. She's trying her very best to look interested in you and it's drawing precious energy away from her brain. Be patient.

## Resting bitch face

Mum has had a rough night and she's in a mood. There's nothing more to say. She hates life today. Nothing will fix it except a four-hour nap. Fussing and whining can be expected.

Note: the resting bitch face is not necessarily directed at anyone in particular. Mother Teresa would cop a bit of attitude if she walked in the door right now. Although she probably deserves it because WE GET IT TESS, YOU'RE PERFECT. I'M TRYING, OKAY?

## Yelling

When a baby starts to grizzle, it's time to put her to bed. When a mother starts to grizzle, it's best to step back and let her go. She hates anyone and everyone who looks at her, speaks to her or drives near her. This may be coupled with jerky movements and incoherent screeching.

It is likely she will be shovelling old Easter eggs into her mouth because she needs sugar like she needs air and she doesn't even care if the chocolate is all chalky and white. STOP STARING.

Do not try to reason with her or argue with her and for the love of god DO NOT tell her to 'calm down' or 'relax'. If you think this is okay to do, you deserve everything you get.

## Crying

As we all know, crying = overtired. A crying mother has tipped over into self-pity and the world is her enemy.

That sad ad on TV? Tears.

Husband taking toast from her plate? Sobbing.

Poonami just as she's walking out the door? Whimpering.

Trying to unlock the car but accidentally hitting the lock button over and over again? Wailing. And swearing.

Tread carefully because being too nice to her could bring her undone completely. Ignore the tears in her eyes and keep talking to her like she's completely sane.

# Zombie

This shell of a woman is one slow blink away from unconsciousness. She cannot respond to your questions. She can't even muster the energy to cry. She can only stare into space. All her energy is being poured into remaining upright and keeping her eyes somewhere near her baby in the hopes she may be able to react before he chokes on his rattle.

Don't take it personally if she shows no enthusiasm for anything you are saying. If she's making eye contact, take it as a sign of interest; she just has no energy to arrange the rest of her face into a socially acceptable expression.

# 43

# What doesn't kill you . . .

What you need to know about tiredness is: it gets better. And I don't mean because your child will start sleeping through the night at three weeks old.

Six-day-old babies don't pick up on routines. Two-week-old babies don't form bad habits from being fed to sleep. Four-week-old babies shouldn't be sleeping for eight hours straight every night. They need to eat. They're tiny and they can't go that long without food.

People who tell you their six week old is doing a twelve-hour sleep stint are bald-faced liars. Or they're drugging their children. Or it happened once because they were so rat-faced delirious with exhaustion they fell into an unconscious slumber and didn't hear their baby crying, so they believe their baby slept all night, and so they will tell everyone they meet, as evidence of their amazing parenting skills. It will drive them to the brink of insanity when it never happens again, but at least they've been able to make everyone else feel bad.

New mothers will fantasise about the elusive block of three-hours-straight sleep. They think about it like they think about Ryan Reynolds's abs. The promise of a four-hour block is simply too much to even think about—too delicious, too life-changing. It's best to keep those dreams realistic.

So no, you won't suddenly start getting huge chunks of sleep just yet. What *will* happen is that you'll get used to it. You'll start to feel less dead. You'll learn you can actually function on two and a half hours' sleep a night. You can stand up. You can hold a conversation. You can even leave your home.

Turns out you won't die from lack of sleep. You might get close, but you will survive.

# 44

# . . . Makes you stronger

People underestimate mothers. They think we're weak and feeble.

Fallacy. Mothers are WARRIORS.

Mothers can survive being torn in half and not die. We can bleed for weeks and not die. We can stay awake for days and not die.

Mothers are put through physical tests most men would crumble at. And yet we survive—nay, we THRIVE.

We keep moving forward, we keep creating life, we keep working and earning and organising everything in everyone's life and we do it with style and class. On no sleep or proper food.

My body has conditioned itself to operate on less than two hours of sleep a night. I've become nocturnal. I could become a soldier of fortune, hunting people by night, fighting in the blackness, sleeping for minutes at a time . . . they'd never catch me.

But if they did catch me, I could withstand weeks of interrogation. Months, even. I've been interrogated for three years straight by my son #blessed. There isn't a question I haven't heard and avoided.

If they moved to negotiation? Ha! I've been dealing with extremists for years #preciousmemories. I have negotiation skills that would put the UN to shame. I could bring together warring nations with the skills I've learnt at dinnertime alone.

And if they moved onto torture, I'd be just fine. I have learnt to cope with the aggressively irritating *woo woo* siren noise my son makes when he wants my attention. It's hardened me. I'm stronger because of it. If I can withstand that, I can withstand anything.

I'm so grateful my children like to scream at the same time, while I'm trying to make dinner, one of them trying to climb my leg while I'm holding a pot of boiling water while someone else spills their drink all over the couch. They've made me a weapon. I'm unstoppable.

We are warriors. Just imagine what we could achieve with a full night's rest.

# 45

# Baby, you are why I'm here

Of course, the one thing that will get you through every day is your baby.

Those tiny little toes, that velvety bottom, the pips and squeaks, the clenched-up fists. Even in the hardest moments, mothers have the ability to pull from a reserve of strength that drives them to do everything they can to protect their babies.

Being a new mum makes you understand that animalistic mother's instinct for the first time. Often, before you even feel love, you'll feel the urge to protect. Taking care of your baby is something you do even when you don't know what else to do. Your baby's needs now come before your own. Every time. You could be exhausted, emotional, irrational and cranky, but when that baby cries, you will get up and go to her, because you are a mother, and *mothers DO*.

That tiny little body resting on your chest will awaken a part of your soul you didn't know was sleeping. Your body will feel empty and lost when that tiny babe isn't in your arms, like you've grown a new limb and being without it puts you off balance.

It's a heady mix of feeling needed, feeling vital, and feeling whole—all at the same time.

It's corny and clichéd and we try not to say it out loud because it would make everyone's eyes roll back down their throats. But . . . having a baby makes you feel like you have a new purpose. Maybe not straightaway. Maybe not for a few months. But one day you'll look down at that tiny person and think, 'Oh, so *this* is the meaning of life, then? *You* are why I'm here. All this time . . . I've been waiting for you.'

# 46

# The stink of motherhood

The 'poo life' it is.

Now you have a newborn, you will find that inspecting, discussing, Googling and comparing human faeces is a perfectly acceptable way to spend your time.

When your partner misses out on a nappy change, a full debrief is held on return. What colour was it? Was it runny? How much was there? How far up his back did it go? How much did you get under your fingernails?

Your baby's first poo—the Vegemite one—is a sight to behold and one you'll never forget, but then it changes. It's yellow and liquid and it has the ability to travel anywhere and everywhere you don't want it to. Everything you own will end up out in the sun because sunlight is the only thing that gets those stains out (actual tip right there).

I once cut my daughter's outfit right off her body because the disaster zone was so extensive, I knew there was no other way to avoid giving her a faecal facial.

I've since learnt that baby clothes with the envelope neckline are designed so you can pull them down over their shoulders to get them off (second actual tip—I'm on a roll).

But newborn baby poo doesn't smell as bad as you think it will. All those hilarious videos of men gagging at the unwrapping of a baby turd? LIES.

Babies' hands. That is the stench you need to know about: the smell of blue cheese wafting from those clenched little fists.

Despite regular baths, babies will become more and more rotten until the day you pry open those tiny clamped hands and find the source of the evil: the unidentifiable white creamy substance inside those paws. How long has it been there? Nobody knows. Since their hands formed in the womb? It's anyone's guess, but it's putrid. And cleaning that stuff out is a chore when those fingers only understand fighting mode. Digging that gunk out of those folds is disgusting and satisfying and necessary.

That other smell? That's you, babe. That's the permanent stench of sour milk coming off you.

# 47

# Guilt and worry

Motherhood brings wonder and beauty to your life, it's true, but there's also a darkness that comes, that no one warns mothers about. Like a smudge on your glasses, that stops you from ever really seeing the splendour in full colour.

It's called guilt and worry: the dark cloud duo, casting a shadow on your heart from hereon in. There's nothing you can do but accept them, because they're side effects of love.

The guilt comes from your desperate desire to be the best mother you can be for your beloved child. You'll want to be a 'super mum' and you'll be bombarded with advice and the arbitrary standards society expects you to achieve and you'll fall short, over and over again, because you're human, and perfection is impossible.

But you'll still try. Because your baby deserves it. Because you love her so wildly, you'll feel angry at yourself for not being better at it. Never in your life have you wanted to be so good at something.

And it will feel like everyone is watching and waiting for you to stuff it all up.

The trick here is to accept that perfection isn't just impossible; it's unnecessary. Martyrdom isn't a requirement of motherhood, even if Janet from that 'Slow Home Schooling' blog wrote a whole article about it. What you need to know is that kids are awfully forgiving as long as you're 'pretty good', most of the time.

But then there's the worry. When you have something this precious, you have so much more to lose.

It might have started in pregnancy when you began to imagine every dark and twisted thing that could go wrong. Then your baby arrived and you've suddenly become aware of how dangerous and filthy the whole world is. Every single living thing is out to damage you and your child. You'll whip yourself into a state every time your baby wheezes or sneezes or poops in a weird colour. You'll open Google and you won't close it again until your kids move out of home.

I once showed a paediatrician a video of my son, fretting and pacing while he watched it. As it finished, I asked what was wrong with my child.

'And, um ... what is it exactly that I should be noticing?' he asked cautiously.

'That weird way he's talking!' I cried. 'You see the way he's trying to make babbling noises but he's doing it with his mouth shut? That's not normal, is it?'

He gave me that look doctors give first-time mums. You know the one where they're trying to decide if you're an overanxious mother or simply a bit slow?

'He's just fine,' he said, in a careful tone that told me he'd decided I was one of the slow ones.

It wasn't the first and certainly won't be the last time I've worried over something ridiculous when it comes to my children.

I've worried I worry too much and I've worried that I don't worry enough. I've also worried that my worries are not quite sane.

I've Googled things like:

- 'Does my child hate the flavour of my milk?'
- 'What shape should baby poo be?'
- 'Will my baby be stunted if he doesn't sleep enough?'
- 'Can you die from sleep deprivation?'
- 'Is my baby a psychopath?'

Motherhood has a way of supercharging the imagination. You can see the worst possible outcome of every situation. Your mind will take you to some dark places, my friend. A simple climb up the stairs could suddenly turn into a life-or-death scenario. See that garbage truck on the street outside your home? What if your child was outside and ran in front of it? I mean, sure, your child is two weeks old, can't even find her own hand and the front door is securely locked, but WHAT IF?

Walking down the footpath with your toddler, for example, leaves you thinking, 'He could trip and fall into oncoming traffic and end up flattened and I'll have to throw myself in front of the next car in grief and then we'll both be on tonight's news and my husband will be a tragic widower until he finds someone really beautiful who never nags and always makes lovely dinners for him and they start a new family and forget all about us and he even takes our photo out of his wallet so he doesn't upset his new wife and only my mother and father will continue to mourn us until they die and then our memory will be gone forever.' For example.

It might just be a flash in the back of your mind, like a quick glimpse into an alternate universe, but there's a constant nagging that your child is incredibly impermanent.

# 48

# You'll probably injure your child

The worrying isn't made better when you yourself are the reason your child is hurt.

This is going to happen and you need to get comfortable with it now. There's a 99 per cent chance you will injure your baby. Not on purpose, of course, but they're slippery, jittery little suckers and eventually you're going to make a dent.

The main areas of threat are:

- cutting fingers while clipping fingernails
- hitting heads on door frames/car doors
- dropping phones on bodies/heads.

Fingernails are probably the first hurdle. Your newborn will come equipped with a set of wolverine claws and the intent to use them on you and himself.

If you think sadomasochists are intense, wait until you have a newborn in your arms who seems determined to claw out his own eyes and draw blood from his own cheeks. It's disturbing. Then you try to latch that little beast and your boobs suffer a torturous death by paper cuts.

So you decide to cut your baby's talons.

I don't like to give advice, but if I did, I'd tell you to let someone else do it the first time. Your baby won't remember but *you* will never recover from the tidal wave of regret and grief when you slice into your child's tender new fingers. And MAN can those things bleed! Best give that special milestone to your partner, mother, sister or random midwife to deal with.

And then there's the moment you give your precious newborn a suspected head injury. When you're carrying a child who won't be put down, all day long, you tend to think of them as part of your body. But they're not part of you so you don't always account for their body parts when walking around.

What I'm saying is: it's not really your fault if their unfused skull accidentally connects with a door frame.

Dropping your phone on the baby probably *is* your fault, though. Then again, you need to take photos of them when they're sleeping because when they're awake they pull that weird gassy face all the time and it's just not as cute as the sleeping face. And taking that sleeping shot from above is much more Instagram-worthy. You know how the 'Gram loves a flat lay. Shame about your baby's flat face, though.

Look, don't feel too bad. They'll injure you right back—breast-feeding neck, baby wrist, post-pregnancy back. Your body will be twisted, pulled and strained because of this kid. I've pulled a stomach muscle from lugging my kid around on my hip. I've damaged a shoulder trying to pick one up.

Soon enough, you'll be at the mercy of a baby who'll headbutt you, kick and slap you and throw things at your face. All out of love, of course.

# 49

# Are you a special kind of moron?

'First-time mum?' they say, with their head tilted and condescension in their eyes. The slight pursing of their lips and the furrow of their brows tell you everything you need to know. With just three words, that doctor or child health nurse will dismiss every concern a new parent might have.

You're hysterical. You're being dramatic. There's nothing wrong but you know nothing about anything so here you are, wasting everyone's time.

The baby brain lingers, it's true, but you're not an idiot, no matter what they say.

The doubt will creep in. You'll stop taking your child to the doctor because you don't want to be told, yet again, that your baby is fine.

What these doctors and nurses are doing is gaslighting you. They're making you believe *you* are the problem, so you're now questioning your own judgement and sanity.

No, you are not a doctor (unless of course, you are, in which case, well done!) but that doesn't mean you don't know when something is wrong with your child. You have every right to ask for attention if your gut is telling you your baby needs it.

So I'm telling you this: you are not a moron. You're not hysterical. You're not a hypochondriac. You know your child better than anyone and you have the right to ask for attention.

You deserve a second opinion. Even if it's just so two people can tell you there's nothing to worry about. No harm has ever been done by getting a second opinion, but a lot of harm can be done when one arrogant doctor dismisses a mother's concerns and sends a sick child home.

# 50

# Opinions and advice: part 2

They'll come from your family, your friends, strangers on the internet, old ladies at the shops, joggers in the park ... literally anyone who lays eyes on you and your baby will want to tell you how you should be doing things.

Deep down, everyone believes a new mother is desperately clueless and in need of instruction. So they'll offer it even when you're coping just fine.

What this does is it makes a mother doubt herself. She starts ignoring her instincts and makes decisions based on what other people are telling her.

So whenever I hear a mum talking about her baby with that edge in her voice that tells everyone she's about one quarter of a coffee away from spontaneous combustion, I can't help but wonder if the problem she's having is actually a problem or if it's just something she thinks needs to be fixed because someone else said so.

Is the fact that baby Bobby falls asleep on your chest every night an actual problem for you or is it because of all the Barbaras out there tutting at your inability to put your kid down DROSWY BUT AWAKE?

Or is it goddamn Indigoh from mother's group with her soul child Samryellia giving you side-eye about your baby's bottle habit because darling Samryellia only drinks dew from the morning leaves so she keeps passing on articles from the Natural News about the deadly effects of cow's milk?

Are you in a state because YOU want things to change or because you think you're *supposed* to?

You know what Ethel would say? Ethel who's 80 years old and raised seven kids single-handedly during the war with no washing machine and a husband who did six minutes of face time with the kids each day. Well she might give you advice on when to start your infant on brandy and how cracking skulls together is an effective discipline technique—BUT, she'd also say, SCREW EVERYONE ELSE. She never had to put up with the opinions of every arsehole in the country every time she fed her kids fried chicken for dinner. She just bloody got on with it and did WHAT WORKED FOR HER.

So if you think you're supposed to be teaching your child to fall asleep alone while also mourning the feeling of that precious baby lying on your chest, SCREW EVERYONE ELSE. Nothing in this world feels better than a sleeping baby in your arms, so don't worry about what everyone else says—do what works for you and what makes you happy. Unless you really genuinely want to change how you parent, stop listening to everyone else. They don't have your child. Remember, it's not a problem unless it's a problem for YOU.

And then there's the useless opinions of random strangers who'll judge every move you make even though it has LESS THAN NOTHING TO DO WITH THEM.

It always comes in the form of 'innocent questions'.

'Is that okay for THE BABY?' they implore, when they see you lifting a coffee to your lips.

'Sure it's great for the baby because it means I don't fall down the stairs while holding him out of sheer exhaustion and my inability to keep my eyes open,' you reply.

'But what about your breast milk? Isn't that caffeine getting through to THE BABY?'

'I'm bottle-feeding.'

*Complete stranger drops dead from heartbreak*

People will care deeply that you're out and about already because shouldn't the baby be at home, away from all these germs?

Oh, but what about that mum who hasn't even made it out of the house yet? She must be struggling big time.

Oh dear, look at that new mum, creeping around her house in silence like an idiot. Doesn't she know babies love a bit of noise? It calms them!

Gah, why is that mother here at this loud play centre? It's too noisy for the baby!

Oh my god, this mother is such a whinger, it's not that hard to get out of the house with a newborn!

Who does she think she is, pretending like it's so easy to just walk out of the house? Has she even packed her baby bag properly?

Is she seriously going out without her child already? Who's going to watch the baby!?

Why can't she ever put that kid down? Is she going to let the daddy have a turn yet?

My advice is to get used to it and to work on your best deadpan, 'eat a wang' face.

# 51

# Your rig has been rejigged

People might have told you this but you probably didn't listen. Or you thought they might be just talking about some stretch marks or some extra junk in your gunty area.

But no—it's everywhere and everything. Occasionally, if you are a unicorn woman made of sunshine and sparkles, you might escape with a bit of boob shrinkage and maybe a bellybutton that can't quite decide whether it's an innie or an outie. But honey, let's be honest. You're not a unicorn, are you? You're a mortal human with skin that's not made of elastic and muscles that will never quite fit back where they used to.

Your skin might sag, your pigmentation might flare up, your boobs will never sit that high again, your hair will start to fall out in fistfuls (don't worry, it grows back eventually. In tufts and sideburns and a furry halo that lasts for a year or two. Super cute!) and your pelvic floor might leak in protest every time you laugh, cough, sneeze, jump, run, squat . . . trampolines are no longer for you.

BUT IT'S OKAY.

I'm not going to lie. The knowledge that your rig has rejigged and can't be jigged back together again? Well, that can be a hard jig to dig.

Women are constantly told to fix themselves. What we need to tell women is: your body won't ever be the same, *but it'll be okay*. Some women's bodies will snap back to their pre-baby size in a few weeks. It doesn't make them freaks and it doesn't make them dangerous; it's sometimes just a matter of genes. After my first baby my stomach was completely flat in two days. Sure, it wobbled and lurched whenever I moved, like an uncooked cake, but it was flat. My arse, however . . .

For most mums, it'll take a bit longer to get their waistline back and much, much longer before they fit into their old clothes. Maybe six months, maybe twelve. If you just let your body do its thing and get back to feeling normal when it's ready, you might just find you don't really care anyway.

Because you know who really, really, *really* doesn't care what your body looks like? Your baby. Not even the tiniest bit. Couldn't even tell you what your body looks like compared to everyone else. You're just Mum and you're amazing in every way.

True story: one day, when my son was about three, I went to pick him up from day care. As soon as I walked in, his educator pounced on me. You could tell she'd been waiting all afternoon to tell me something he'd done, so I knew it was going to be amazing.

She'd been asking the kids to describe their mums. Some of the kids said their mums looked like princesses; some said their mums looked like angels.

She turned to my boy. 'What does *your* mummy look like?'

My son: 'A rectangle.'

# 52

# The textbook baby

Once upon a time there was a little baby who was perfect. The baby was in a solid sleep routine from the day she came home from the hospital. At two weeks old, she learnt, after crying for exactly five minutes, that it was best to settle herself, go to sleep and stay asleep. She fed every three hours. She slept in the middle of the living room because she felt soothed by the sounds of her family as they went about their day around her. She loved tummy time so very much and she couldn't wait to taste a wide range of healthy foods.

This baby lived in a textbook.

This baby *doesn't exist in real life*. This baby is designed to make you feel like you're doing it all wrong. This baby is a SCAM.

I have a theory that this baby was created by a man in order to demoralise and destroy a mother's self-confidence so she would stay at home in shame, marinate in her failure and keep a clean house.

No babies will follow the textbook. They're not great at remembering things at this age. Your routine might be airtight but your newborn can't figure out how to look at things with both eyes yet, so it's probably not going to ruin his day if you read a book *before* bath time instead of *after*.

You can't train or spoil newborns. They're basically potatoes with eyes—eyes that can barely see you. Please don't punish yourself if your newborn can only sleep in a pitch-black room in complete silence, on your chest, while you stand for hours at a time. He's not 'learning bad habits'. He's still trying to figure out how to be alive.

It is, of course, totally possible you'll get a textbook baby—they have to base their stories on someone don't they? They are mythical and beautiful, like unicorns—but if you get one, don't go boasting just yet.

A Unicorn Baby is a result of pure luck, not a supernaturally talented parent. But this doesn't stop parents of the Unicorn Baby from rubbing this in everyone's face. The obnoxious humblebrag is a sin carried out by sanctimummies called Brogany, and the universe will eventually punish them with the four-month sleep regression.

The only people allowed to humblebrag are parents of three or more children who have had successive jerk babies and have finally scored a unicorn. They deserve their moment in the sun. Let them have it.

# 53

# Goodbye to the old you

You've been a human beanbag for a tiny person for weeks and weeks on end. You've learnt how to go to the toilet while holding a child, you've changed nappies in the boot of the car, you've said no to countless invitations and you've learnt to survive on 90 minutes of sleep snatched throughout the day and night.

It has been *sacrifice* since the moment that child was handed to you.

And you're spent.

In the dark of the night, when you're feeding this bottomless pit of a child, struggling to stay upright, you will realise there's no end to this. It's like you hadn't ever considered it before but here you are, finally realising what should have been the most obvious part of motherhood: it's constant. Relentless. Incessant. Permanent. You never ever get to clock off. Your ability to be selfish has been taken away and you never realised how much you'd miss it.

You wanted this baby; you're over the moon that she's here. You love her more than you thought possible. And yet you want a break. You get annoyed that she wants you all the time. You want to leave your house on a whim. You want to go drinking with your friends. You want your body to be just yours. Just once.

You think about what you were doing a couple of months ago and you feel . . . Pain? Sadness? Grief? The old you has gone and she's not coming back. You're never going to be that person again. You know you have to let go of who you were but you didn't even get to say goodbye.

When you do let her go, things will start to change within you.

Your baby pounds an angry fist against your chest and you brush the back of her hand with one finger and it calms her. She gives a little shudder-sigh, which you know, without even looking, means she's fallen asleep. You pull her to your face to kiss her velvet cheek and a tear falls from your eye as you let the last bit of the past crumble away.

Because this is you now. You know this baby. She knows you. And you need each other. Through the endless nights, the frustrated tears and the small wins you've had, you've become a mother. You almost didn't notice it happening. You realise that all your thoughts are about her. You put her first, without even thinking about it. You know you'd die for this tiny, needy little creature. Despite all of it, you wouldn't go back.

All the tiny pieces of your soul have been scattered to the wind but slowly, surely, they've settled to the ground and, bit by bit, they've come together. You're different now—more beautiful, more complicated, but stronger. You're a mother.

# 54

# 24 hours with a newborn

Let's start at 5 a.m. Not because it's the start of your day. There is no start to your day. There is no end. It's just one never-ending, mind-melting continuum of time from the minute you come home from the hospital until . . . I honestly don't know, sorry.

## 5 a.m.

You've been sleeping for 40 glorious minutes when you are woken by the bleating of your baby in the bassinet next to you. You swear you fed her about fifteen seconds ago. You're pretty sure your left eyeball is bleeding because when your eyes have been open non-stop for three weeks they start to peel and crack from exposure to the elements.

You stick your baby on your boob. It used to hurt like a mother but your nipples are now completely numb because the cluster-feeding has toughened them into a pair of leather coasters. Your nipples are now like the soles of Tarzan's feet. You could climb a palm tree with those boobs.

You try really hard not to fall asleep on the baby, drift off for a few seconds and wake in terror, swinging your arms wildly trying to find the baby, panicking that you've just suffocated her with your obscene boobs.

Locate the baby, who is still attached to your boob, and breathe a sigh of relief because you are a wonderful mum who will never sleep with your baby in the bed because it's so dangerous.

Close your eyes for two seconds.

Wake up 90 minutes later.

WHERE'S THE BABY?! Oh. Right there. Still on your boob, sound asleep and sucking away at what now looks like an empty plastic bag. Meanwhile, your other boob is a watermelon, leaking milk all down your pyjama pants.

Try to pull the baby off your footy-sock boob, i.e. unleash the beast.

## 6.45–7.30 a.m.

Rocking, shushing, patting, bouncing, walking, singing, begging, pleading, cajoling, crying (both of you) . . .

## 7.30 a.m.

Finally put baby down and creep out in a sideways ninja crab manoeuvre so the baby can't sense the shift in atmospheric pressure as you depart. Pull the door shut so slowly you're not sure it's actually moving, but don't make a sound because despite all the books saying newborns love a bit of background noise, you appear to have the only baby in existence who wakes to the sound of dust mites munching their way through the bedsheets.

Shuffle silently towards the shower and step under the sweet, sweet relief of scalding hot water.

Immediately turn shower off because you hear the baby cry.

Nope, false alarm. Turn the shower back on.

WAIT! That's totally a baby crying . . . Nope. Still no cry. STOP!

Continue this excruciating game until the hot water runs out and you've wasted half of nap time. You didn't even get to wash your hair. (It's now day seven of dry shampoo.)

Consider popping on a pair of jeans and a nice top but before you realise what's happening you've donned a clean pair of pyjamas. It's for the best.

Creep back to check on the baby, who looks like a sleeping angel.

Feel your heart swell with love and pride, right as the baby lets rip with a gut-churning fart.

Watch her little eyes snap open and her arms and legs shoot out in fright.

Dissolve into fits of hysterical, delirious laughter because watching a baby wake herself up with her own fart is the funniest thing you've ever seen. Then burst into tears because the baby is now awake—and pissed.

# 7.45 a.m.

Try to wrestle furious child onto your boob. She comes at you with a gnashing mouth and wild eyes and you have a brief moment of terror because it looks like a tiny T-rex is about to devour your chest.

Flop onto the couch and let her fall asleep on the boob even though you know you're not supposed to do that because it's a sleep crutch and she'll need to be fed to sleep until she's fifteen years old and you'll never get a full night's sleep again and she'll probably become a narcissist but you figure you can break the habit some other day. Right now you just want to sit and enjoy the silence.

Look lovingly at your baby and notice her scalp is moving. HOLY MOTHER OF GOD.

Google 'pulsating fontanelle'.

All is okay. Perfectly normal.

Close your eyes for ten minutes and then feel guilty because surely you should be gazing lovingly into your baby's eyes, or lying her on the floor for tummy time, or reading Shakespeare and listening to Chopin because you've read that you need to provide an enriching and stimulating environment or you'll condemn your little snowflake to a life of mediocrity and disappointment.

Google 'fine motor skills activities for newborns'.

Discover your three week old still doesn't know how to pick things up and realise you are a complete failure. Open a therapy bank account in your baby's name. Wonder how often she'll talk about you in her sessions.

## 8.30 a.m.

Lay baby down so you can have a brain-building chat with her. Realise you have nothing at all to say, then realise that's okay because it seems she's perfectly content to stare at the ceiling fan. Feel slightly rejected. She really likes that fan.

Enjoy the brief silence before the air is ripped apart by a guttural symphony that sounds and smells like a blocked sewer bursting. Marvel at how unconcerned the baby seems to be about sitting in a pool of her own scum.

Pick up the baby only to discover that the carnage is EVERY-WHERE. Curse the nappy for not doing its job. Curse the outfit for being so white. Curse Mother Nature for only giving you two hands. It's surely a design flaw.

## 9.30 a.m.

Disinfect kitchen sink.

Google 'washed baby's bum in kitchen sink + baby poo + food preparation areas + infection risk'.

## 10.30 a.m.

Baby has been asleep for twenty whole minutes. Switch on kettle. Baby wakes immediately.

Feed her again.

## 11.30 a.m.

You've spent 40 minutes trying to put baby back down for a sleep. She is screaming so hard she stops breathing a few times. Scream back at baby to BREATHE GODDAMN YOU! Acknowledge that might have been a step too far. Recognise you're up against a master of manipulation. Accept defeat.

Start tearing your place apart, looking for the dummy your Aunty Marg gave you at your baby shower. You didn't want it (nipple confusion, teeth issues, etc.). But you're starting to think it couldn't hurt for a couple of weeks, right? So long as you only let her use it when she's really upset. And never, ever in public. Obviously.

Tear open the pack and stick it right in her mouth. Then realise you didn't sterilise it and frantically pull it back out, but it's too late. You've infected her for sure. And now she's screaming even harder. Run the dummy under hot water with one hand while jiggling screaming baby with the other and try to reason with yourself that babies in rural Afghanistan don't get sterilised dummies. Ignore the small voice telling you that babies in rural Afghanistan also die.

Google 'unsterilised dummy'.

Google 'nipple confusion'.
Google 'breaking the dummy habit'.
Google 'babies in rural Afghanistan'.

## 12.30 p.m.

Baby is asleep. Finally make yourself some breakfast. Hello, Nutella on toast! You'll have time for nutritionally sound meals soon. Right?

You could do some of that laundry but you pick up a book. Read the first page eight times. Still have no idea what it's about. Decide to just watch TV.

Before you pick up the remote you check on the baby. She's very quiet and very still. You're not entirely sure she's breathing. Dangle precariously over her face, trying to hear her breathe. Consider getting a mirror to hold in front of her nose.

A piece of your hair falls and smacks her right in the face.

Feed baby.

## 1.30 p.m.

Consider going for a walk in the fresh air.

Spend one hour packing, preparing, double-checking and dressing.

Go to push pram out the front door at the exact moment the baby poos herself, her clothes and the pram bassinet. Burst into tears and decide you'd really rather watch TV anyway.

## 2.30–6.30 p.m.

Sit on couch. Feed baby. Watch TV. Repeat.

Take hundreds of cute photos of baby on phone so you can send to the grandparents and tell them all how marvellously you're coping.

# 6.30 p.m.

Husband comes home. Hand child over and go and hide in the pantry so you can eat biscuits in silence while he bathes the baby. Feel slightly pissed off that the baby is happy and quiet for her daddy.

Google 'how to tell if your baby hates you'.

# 7.30–10.30 p.m.

Feed baby. Try to put her down for bedtime but realise you could spend two hours settling her in a dark room or you could just hold her on your chest while you sit next to your husband, having 'us time', which is actually just sitting silently next to each other watching TV and trying not to fall asleep.

# 10.30 p.m.–5 a.m.

Crawl into bed and 'go to sleep', which is code for 'have a series of short, barely useful naps in between feeds and nappy changes in the dark while husband snores blissfully beside you'.

# 5 a.m.

Good morning!

# Part three
# Babyhood

or

*Who even am I?*

*Dear Baby Mama,*

*On the other side of the murky, dark, muddled newborn days is babyhood. It's a slow step out into the sunshine, where sleeping patterns are formed, neck muscles are built, and a new rhythm to life is discovered. At about three months in, you'll start to feel like maybe, just maybe, you'll survive this.*

*Babies are the best. People don't celebrate them enough. They're the perfect humans. They're chill, they're happy, they can't talk, they can't walk, and they think you're spectacular #givemeallthebabies.*

*But parents with babies can be insufferably self-satisfied. They start mummy blogs, they hand out advice to parents with older kids, they roll their eyes at people who say raising kids is hard. They refer to themselves as 'Mummy' and 'Daddy', and their little muffin smiles all day long, naps for two hours at a time and is happy with a paper plate and a song.*

*They're completely oblivious to how obnoxious their status updates about the angel baby are—#blessed #grateful #lovebeinghermum #borntobeamother—or that photo album with 82 shots of their first day at the beach in which they've tagged everyone they've ever known because surely they'd all want to see?*

*Ah, babies—so perfect!*

*Until they're not.*

*Karma gets these people eventually. It comes out of the blue, sending smug mummies (smugmies? smugummies? smumgs?) hurtling towards the internet with a wine bottle as they try to figure out what leap their snowflake is going through right now.*

*Welcome to motherhood, where one day you're Martha bloody Stewart and the next you're Roseanne Barr. It's not your fault: trust me. It's your child. They're all jerks now and then.*

*But don't worry, babies are mostly beautiful, agreeable, social little monkeys that you'll want to show off to the world. It's time to step out into civilisation, reconnect with other humans and find your groove as a MUM.*

*The problem is, once you start looking out to the world, you'll inevitably start to compare. You'll see women on social media who go to the gym every day, dress their babies in bespoke linen rompers and set up sensory activities before they go to bed so they're ready to go in the morning. They write wildly successful blogs during nap time and have created their own line of empowering T-shirts. They also seem to have professional photographers following them around, taking #candid snaps of them looking #blessed in their impeccably styled, Scandi-neutral playrooms #beige.*

*Their baby bags are organisational masterpieces with tiny satchels and compartments for every item they could ever need. When are they doing all this organising? Your baby bag is half supply closet–half garbage dump. It contains: one crumpled nappy, three bottles of water, four half-empty packets of baby wipes, a box of sultanas, seventeen used tissues, a dozen receipts and a pooey nappy from that time you changed your kid on the floor of a shopping centre change room because there wasn't a change table and then you shoved the dirty nappy back in your bag to avoid putting it in the shop's bin because that's rude, but now you're walking around with human faeces inside your bag. There's also, inexplicably, a peg.*

*Everyone else's kids seem to be sleeping through the night, they're identifying colours, they're taking first steps at eight months old. Your kid . . . isn't. All these mums are starting businesses, doing motivational speaking tours and seem surrounded by hoards of equally stylish mum friends. You . . . aren't.*

*It's okay, it's going to take some time and a bit of effort but you and your garbage dump bag will find your feet—and your mum tribe—and you will survive this.*

*Love Lauren xx*

# 55

# Mum friends

In a small brown room, wallpapered with posters for meningo-coccal vaccinations and breastfeeding classes, a circle of women sat on green plastic chairs, cradling their brand-new babies, hoping everyone could see how well they were coping.

The smiles were fixed, and appearances were being kept, until the voice of one brave woman cut through.

'This is really hard,' she said. 'Why didn't anyone tell us it would be this *hard*?'

Her white flag was an amnesty for the group, giving us the freedom to tell the truth.

'Oh but they *did* tell us,' I replied. 'We just didn't *believe* them.'

The laugh that followed was the tipping point, the moment we all stopped pretending. We exhaled the effort and expectation, the unrealistic standards and fear. We looked at each other for what felt like the first time, and we started talking.

My son was eight weeks old, and I was skating along the top of a very dark spiral, feeling alone and unsure, wondering why I wasn't more content, why I didn't love motherhood more. I loved my child, but the day-to-day grind was getting me down. I worried I wasn't cut out for motherhood.

That first meeting with my mothers' group changed everything for me. Those women saved me from that spiral.

Six years, a second round of kids and the formation of a 'dads' group' later, these are the best women I know. (They were very forceful about their inclusion in this book.)

They're open and honest and they get me. They've never needed me to clarify how much I adore my children whenever I complain.

These women are the people I can message, saying ABOUT TO MURDER MY CHILDREN, WHO WILL GIVE ME AN ALIBI? And they'll all write back giving me various backstories for where we were when it happened.

They know how much I love my kids but they also know that sometimes you need to say and think really dark things to get you through the day.

They are my people. *You need your people.*

Men don't get it. It's not their fault. Men can be amazing partners and exceptional fathers . . . but they can't be mums. They'll simply never be able to understand what you're going through like another mum can.

Being a first-time mum can be so much lonelier than you thought. Despite spending all day, every day with a small person, you can feel completely isolated from the world. Mum friends are your deliverance. Your emancipation. Your absolution and salvation.

When you've been thrown from the workplace into the motherhood, you're adrift without a team. Who do you compare notes with? Who can you bitch about the boss with? Who can cover for you when you need to nip out to the shops?

Humans are team players. We are made to work in groups. So when you bring a baby home, all you really need to survive is a few hours of sleep a day, and people to whinge to. If you get these two things, you'll be A-OKAY.

It can't be your old friends, bless them. They're lovely, I'm sure, but you might find they don't want to hang out with you so much now you've started wearing your husband's trackpants and your preferred topic of conversation is poo, vomit and why your baby won't sleep.

It can't be friends with half a dozen kids. No matter how hard they try not to, those friends will always roll their eyes a bit when you tell them how hard your day was. When you've got more children than limbs, you can't help but think mothers of one child have it easy. Let me be clear, one child is NOT EASY. Not if it's your first.

It needs to be other first-time mums with babies the same age as yours. Absolutely no one will understand all the emotions, the questions, the uncertainty and torturous exhaustion like another mum who's going through the exact same things at the exact same time.

Of course, mums' groups don't always work. Sometimes people who would never normally be friends with each other are thrown together and expected to bond over the shared experience of having a newborn. It's not that simple. But don't give up! Find another mums' group. Stalk women in the playground, find an online group, join a gym and loiter near the babies in the creche until their mums come to pick them up. Whatever you have to do, find some mum friends. Ones that get you. Ones who support you. Ones who bring wine and/or coffee and cake.

# Mums you need to be friends with

## Down-to-earth mums

Rowena doesn't care what sort of bag you're carrying, how you do your hair or how you choose to feed your baby. She just wants to find a cafe with good coffee and highchairs so she can sit and talk about life.

## Storytelling mums

Laura's a hot mess with a kid who doesn't sleep or eat, and she can never get herself out of her house on time, but man, can she tell a good story. She never fails to make you all laugh while making you feel better because you know you're not the only one who struggles.

## Solidarity mums

If you're falling apart, Lucy's the one to grab you by the shoulders and tell you you're okay in a voice that makes you think maybe you will be. She always knows exactly what to say to make you feel stronger and she never makes you feel like your problems are yours alone.

## Chill mums

Your child turns and smacks Erica's child straight across the face and you leap out of your seat to scold him, but Erica just laughs, shrugs and says, 'She'll live.'

Erica always listens to your problems but she never tells you how to fix them. She just nods, smiles and says, 'Yeah, me too, babe.'

## Funny mums

You're sad and stressed and you're feeling like the whole world is against you, so you unload in an essay to your mum friends' message group . . . Sally responds with a gif of a woman being smacked with hot dogs. Sometimes you just need a friend who'll tell you to suck it up with a well-timed gif.

## Mums who love your kids

Whenever you mention something cool your child just did, Nina cheers the loudest and the longest because she loves your child. She never feels the need to compete or compare; she's just genuinely happy for you.

# Mums you don't need to be friends with

## Mums you need to impress

Alana dresses her baby in clothes that cost more than yours, directs your attention to her designer nappy bag every chance she gets and can't believe you didn't get diamond studs like hers for a 'push present'. Alana is very impressed with her things and she needs you to agree. But she's also making you feel embarrassed about the $60 baby bag your mum bought you and you get the feeling she's scoffing at your baby's Target onesie.

Alana is not for you. You don't want to be worrying about meeting anyone else's standards when you're already worried about meeting your own.


## Expert mums

Sarah's doing everything right (according to her) and she wants to fix you and your baby. With. All. The. Advice. You didn't ask for the advice, you don't want the advice, but here she is, asking, 'Have you tried ...?' and forcing a *Save Our Sleep* book onto you because you *simply must*!

Sarah means well, but she won't ever stop trying to tell you how to parent.

## Competitive mums

Lena wants to win and your baby is the loser. Anyone twisted enough to find fault in someone else's child so hers will look better is not a person you need in your life. No one needs the added pressure of someone sweetly and innocently asking you, 'Oh, isn't Rufus rolling yet? Goodness, Milo was rolling weeks ago! I think he's just extra-strong, you know?' What you need is the mum who's going to say, 'Yeah, Cooper's rolling but he hasn't found his hands, so I probably won't contact the AIS just yet.'

## Judgemental mums

- The subtle: 'Oh, you're using *dummies*, are you? How interesting! No, *really*—good for you.'
- The backhanded: 'Oh, you're using the Baby Benny carrier? That's a nice colour. I'm using the PostureBaby, of course, because it's the gold-standard carrier for baby's hip development and it's recommended by orthopaedic specialists. But yours is pretty.'
- The to-your-face: 'You're *co-sleeping* with your baby? I don't understand why anyone would do that. It's not safe and you're just teaching your child to be co-dependent.'

# Mums you might want to give a chance

## Overachieving mums

Nicola's already signed up for Baby Pilates, Baby First Aid, GymbaROO and flute lessons for when Henry masters his reach-and-grab. Don't write Nicola off just yet because she brings all the homemade treats and you might be able to get her to calm the farm eventually.

## Panicking mums

Annie's pretty sure her baby should be waving by now and she's got an emergency paediatrician appointment lined up but she'd really love your input on whether she should be worried or not. Should she be doing more? She's just SO tired because she can't sleep at night with all the decisions she has to make every day.

Someone hand Annie a paper bag and give her a cuddle. You might just be the one who can help her relax.

## The dad

Richard turns up now and then just to prove he can do it better than any woman. And he does, the bastard. He's got some good tips for playing with your baby, though, so maybe let him stay.

Most importantly: BE a good mum friend. No one in your life knows what you're going through like these women. Trust them. Be open with them. Don't judge them. Don't try to compete with them. Take the opportunity to be completely vulnerable and admit what you're struggling with. They'll be your biggest support.

# 56

# Parenting is like running

What you *don't* need in your life is condescending older mums who are super fond of saying things like 'Just you wait!' and 'It gets worse!' and, my favourite, 'Little kids, little problems; big kids, big problems'. Ugh, eat a bag of willies, Tina! Thanks for letting me know there's absolutely no light at the end of this tunnel and the next fifteen years of my life are going to suck. Super useful info, thanks!

They might even say something incredibly unhelpful like 'Cherish this while it lasts', which is the last thing you want to hear when you're counting down the days until your kid can wake up, dress himself and deliver a hot coffee to you in bed.

What these women mean is: 'I miss when my child thought I was her whole world because right now she barely looks at me.' Which is fair enough, but what they forget is that when their kids' worlds revolved around them, it was because their kids *needed* them every second of the day. And every second of the night. And every time they were on the toilet or trying to eat dinner or talking on the phone or trying to form one single coherent thought above the screaming.

They forget every bad, hard, exhausting part of parenthood. And even if they don't forget, it seems easy in hindsight because they've been there, done that, and earned the 'Baby' patch on their parenting merit sash.

Older parents have done the training, you see. They've built up their parenting stamina—which they certainly didn't have when they started out.

Because parenting is like running, and when you first become a parent you are a lard-filled sloth person who's just been told to get up and sprint for 200 metres.

If you've never moved your body before, that's going to be really hard, if not impossible. You're just not built to do it.

In that first race, there'll be some people who'll struggle to make it to the finish line. They'll stop at the halfway mark, vomit their guts up, limp over the line and pass out. DONE.

Some people will cope better because they have more favourable conditions. They might have a nice tailwind picking them up and carrying them forward. And just so we don't get too confused here, when I say 'tailwind', I mean a kid who loves to sleep and eat. You know, an egg baby who lets you rest and generally enjoy life.

Eventually, after doing the 200-metre sprint all day, every day, for months on end, it'll start to become easier and you'll begin to feel almost competent.

But then your child will go through a leap or a regression or something—they're always going through *something*—and suddenly, you're not doing the 200 metres anymore. Now you need to run 1500 metres.

That will feel impossible. You'll cry, 'But what about the 200 metres? I can do the 200 metres, no problem!' And all of a sudden, that 200-metre sprint will look like a leisurely stroll.

Over the years the distance will get longer and longer, and every time it changes, it'll feel impossible, but with training, your fitness will improve and you'll find you can cope.

Eventually, you'll find yourself dealing with a sixteen year old who's facing the assault of high school and just generally being a teenager and it's draining for your whole family.

Congratulations! You are now running the marathon.

It's exhausting, it's gruelling, and you feel spent at the end of every day, but you're okay because you're fit and your body can do it. But when you hear people complaining about the 200-metre sprint, you'll want to smack their ignorant, naive little faces.

Which is pretty bloody unfair. By the time your kid is a teen you will have been training for years, while poor old 200-metre mum over there is a bowl of jelly on legs. She's just starting out and it's going to take her just as long as it took you to build up her strength.

If you have two or three kids, and fifteen, sixteen or seventeen years of experience under your belt, you're a professional athlete, my friend. And if you've got kids with a large age gap between them, you're basically a CrossFit athlete, doing the marathon and the sprints at the same time because you're a goddamn champ.

So please remember this when you tell a 200-metre sprinter she shouldn't complain because her race is so much easier than yours.

There are, of course, some really gracious marathon runners out there. They'll freely admit that sprinting and marathon-running are actually very different, and they're pretty open about the fact that they wouldn't go back to sprinting if you paid them.

They'll tell you that yes, marathon running *is* hard but it's not the same as the intense, full-body, all-consuming, lung-busting sprint. They don't miss it, but they'll cheer on the sprinters while hard-passing on ever stepping back onto the short-course track.

Those marathon runners are beautiful people and we need to treasure them and thank them for having the perspective and graciousness to acknowledge that people at different stages of parenting can cope with different levels of intensity.

Then there are the retired runners who don't run anymore but they sit on the sidelines and call out such encouragement as: 'Enjoy that run! Cherish it! It goes so fast!'

They're sitting there reminiscing about their heyday on the track, remembering the wind in their face and the strength in their legs, and they want to know why the younger runners don't embrace the joy of running like *they* used to. They've forgotten the gruelling training, the injuries to the body and the bone-crushing fatigue of the never-ending race.

The longer you go through it, the fitter you get, and the easier it all looks in hindsight.

So, when you've got yourself some miles on the track, please don't compare your fitness to someone who's just strapping on the running shoes. Remember how hard it was when you were going through it. New mums will thank you for it.

# 57

# The milestones

*Is he hitting his milestones?*

   *What milestones has he reached?*

   *Where is he with his milestones?*

   Welcome to the milestone era.

   It's an obsession.

   First smile, first laugh, first wave, first roll, first babble, sitting up, crawling, maybe even those precious first steps . . .

   The exact age, down to the minute, that your baby reaches that milestone feels VITAL.

   My son rolled from his front to his back at about three months old. The average age for this milestone is about four months so, naturally, my child is gifted. Video was taken, status updates were issued; I was skipping with excitement and pride when I went to our next appointment with the paediatrician. 'He can *roll!*' I declared, like a woman who'd just won the Nobel Peace Prize.

   'He probably just fell over,' the doctor said.

   *Pardon?*

He might as well have told me my child was ugly and lacking charisma. I was enraged and affronted. How dare he not acknowledge and appreciate my child's achievement?

To this day I maintain my child DID NOT fall over. He did it twice and with purpose.

Of course, he couldn't clap until he was about eighteen months old. This is at least a year after he should've been able to do it, but let's not dwell on arbitrary milestones, okay? They mean nothing. Who needs to clap, really?

It all comes good in the end. Your baby might not be able to use her pincer grip until months after all her peers are doing it, but you know what? I've never once been asked to display my pincer grip in a job interview.

Personally I think we should be celebrating all sorts of milestones. Here are some *parenthood* milestones you might want to commemorate:

- The first time you scoop a poo out of the bath with your bare hands.
- The first time you scoop baby vomit out of your bra with your bare hands.
- The first time you cut off your baby's outfit to avoid wiping poo all over their face.
- The first time they fall off the couch while you're watching TV.
- The first time you wipe their nose with your bare hands.
- The first time you misplace your baby in your own home.
- The first time your baby bites your nipple and you scare them with your scream.

Some parenting milestones you might want to remember for later on:

- The first time your child repeats a swear word.
- The first time you throw out one of their toys as punishment.
- The first time you say, 'Because I said so'.
- The first time you bribe them to do something.
- The first time you stick your finger up at them behind their back.

Don't forget to take photots for the scrapbook!

# 58

# Things take forever now

Babies take up all your time.

Literally, ALL OF IT. You'll wake up—sorry, your baby will wake up—and you'll spend the whole day hustling, but at the end, you will have achieved absolutely nothing.

Remember when you dreamed about learning a language or scrapbooking your child's first year of life? That won't happen.

You're not being lazy and you're not the only one getting nothing done during the day. It's just not possible.

You might start out your day with a grand plan for some sensory play because you spent four hours on Pinterest last night when you should have been sleeping.

While your baby is eating a piece of toast but not actually swallowing a damn thing, you start to set up a 'small world' tray with little animals and rice and some leaves for trees. It's going to be beautiful and stimulating and you can't wait to take photos for Instagram.

You get as far as taking out the tray and a bag of rice before your child hurls his toast at your hair, leaving a chunk of regurgitated bread clinging to your fringe. As you attempt to wipe the mounds of dough from yourself and the cupboard doors, your child backs out a log so toxic, the stink of it makes your eyes water.

You grab your sweet little darling for a nappy change and the death roll he performs as soon as you take off that nappy spreads excrement up your arm, his back, the wall, the blinds and, inexplicably, the floor outside his room. You're not entirely positive there isn't poo on the fan but you'll deal with that the next time you need to turn it on.

You spend a good twenty minutes deep in poo removal and you think you've nearly finished when you turn and find your child has been keeping busy with the tub of nappy cream. You curse yourself because you should have realised he was too quiet, but you breathe through it, pick up your now fully creamed child and put him straight in the bath where you discover that nappy cream is like indelible lipstick, the stuff that only a special lotion will remove. The nappy cream has turned your baby into a moisture-repelling aquatic creature. The water beads and rolls off him like a duck.

You strip yourself off while he's in the bath because you're now covered in toast, poo and nappy cream and you've got a strict three-dubious-substances-maximum rule for your clothing.

The doorbell rings and you're now convinced the postman is spying on you because he only ever rings the doorbell when you're naked, breastfeeding or trying to get the baby to sleep. You ignore the door even though you know it means you'll have to go to the post office to pick up the package later and that's about as appealing as rubbing Tiger Balm on your eyeballs right now.

You spend the next 45 minutes trying to get clothes on yourself and your child and then realise it's his nap time and you didn't manage to fit in any sensory play at all.

So you spend nap time setting it up for him, as well as cracking out a quick clean of the bathroom and kitchen, which you manage to do in fourteen minutes flat because—surprise!—he's awake again.

You manage to take one passable photo of him holding a tiger, which you will use for Instagram tonight (#smallworldplay) but you won't mention that he upended the entire tray and you spent the afternoon cleaning rice out of the carpet and trying to stop him from eating it before you lost your mind and threw the whole, hateful small world crapshow in the bin.

You might have fantasised about all the hours you'd spend reading and playing with your child but, realistically, babies create work wherever they go. Those special memories you wanted to make will be exciting and special for exactly three and a half minutes before your baby's need to seek and destroy takes over.

It's not that you shouldn't try to make those special memories; it's just that you might want to lower your expectations and not feel defeated if one tiny little moment takes the whole freaking day.

# 59

# But slowing down is good

Sometimes, though, a time-stealing baby is exactly what you need. If you've lived your life on the go—working, partying, socialising, working some more—it might be time to slow down.

Babies often come at a point in your life when you're ready to stop doing all those things people say you'll miss. All those nights out dancing? Yeah, that was starting to get old. The crazy hours at work followed by work dinners? Small talk is the *worst*. Drinking all night and sleeping all day? Well, the sleeping part sounds okay. But the rest of it? Thank god you don't have to pretend you love it anymore.

Now you're at home, sitting on the floor, handing blocks to your baby and you think about how different your life is. And maybe you're okay with that.

Babies can bring softness to your life; a light you didn't realise was missing. If you let them, they'll force you to stop rushing around, trying to accomplish all the things, every day. You can stop, breathe, be slow, potter, feel the breeze, smile, look at the sky, touch the leaves, forget about the world for a moment or two.

While everyone is out there, hurrying about and trying to win at life, you can opt out for a little while. Babies are like the ultimate lesson in mindfulness. Here you are *living* it, one game of peekaboo at a time.

# 60

# Being a successful woman might not make you a successful mum

My twelve-week-old baby had closed his beautiful blue eyes approximately three times in his entire life. I wasn't just tired, I was WIRED. My brain was hurtling around my skull, breaking the sound barrier, and I felt like I was on fast-forward as I arrived early for our second mums' group session at the local health clinic.

I couldn't get into the classroom because the nurses were having a meeting, so I sat down outside, hugging my wide-eyed baby and mentally reviewing everything I'd read about baby sleep in the last couple of months. I thought about all the questions I was going to ask the nurse when the session started. I kicked myself for not bringing a notebook.

As I waited, on that hard plastic chair, rocking the tiny president of the 'Sleep is for Losers' club, I could hear the nurses inside the room having a laugh. They were talking about mothers—specifically the kind of mothers that came to this particular clinic, in a suburb filled with middle-class career women in their thirties.

'These mums are so much harder,' I heard a nurse laugh. *Huh?* My ears pricked up.

'They have to know everything,' said another. 'They overthink everything!'

More laughter.

'Yes!' (Actual cackling now.) 'They treat their babies like their job! They don't listen to their instincts and they panic about EVERYTHING!'

Did I mention how tired I was? I was probably sitting there with my shirt wide open, maternity bra unclipped, a damp breast pad sitting in my lap . . . but through the fog, I was fairly sure I'd just been insulted.

When our class started, I looked around the group of first-time mothers. Almost all of them were in their thirties; almost all of them were successful in their careers. Almost all of them looked a little frazzled, stressed and determined to 'figure out' these strange little creatures and wondering if they'd ever find that elusive 'mother's instinct'.

We spent the first few months of our kids' lives swapping research papers and articles we'd read and sharing reviews of baby products to make sure we were doing everything the 'right way'. We overanalysed every sleep regression, every weird poo, every feed that didn't go to plan.

I started to think those cackling nurses might've been a tiny bit right.

It kinda makes sense. At a certain point in your life, you stop flying by the seat of your pants. You take on responsibility; you make decisions, solve problems, innovate, meet targets and goals. You feel like you have control over your life. You know who you are and where you're going.

But then you have a baby, and suddenly you're at the mercy of the most insubordinate human being ever.

In the workplace, this would definitely be a matter for HR. There'd be a meeting of some sort, possibly an awkward mediation where HR makes you both talk about your needs, the team's needs and your strategies for working together as a cohesive unit.

At the very least, you'd be bitching to your workmates about this little turd who has no respect for seniority.

But there's no HR at home. There's no organisational flow chart to show this kid who's boss. There are no standard operating procedures to follow.

There's just you and a baby who will literally crap on you if he feels like it.

So you try to outsmart this kid by reading every book and article you can find. You figure the answers are there . . . you just need to find them. But the answers just make everything worse.

FAAAARK.

If you're used to being good at things, it might just send you over the edge.

I calmed down, eventually. As I gave up control and stopped trying to rationalise everything, I embraced the lack of rules and structure. I finally understood that there are things I'll never understand. I felt okay about not knowing it all. And it all started to feel a lot more natural, and a LOT more fun.

I found my mother's instinct. It was hiding behind a pile of books.

# 61

# The manual exists

They say there's no manual for parenting, which is utter bull because there are *thousands* of manuals. Not to mention millions of pages on the internet. Any mother with a baby knows the web is heaving with encyclopaedic content on 'how to raise children'.

Let's just say this now, so you don't completely lose your mind in this process: every single thing you read will be contradicted by something else. There is literally *not one thing* you will read about parenthood that doesn't have an opposing opinion out there. Except maybe something like 'Don't give the baby Fanta in a bottle'. I haven't seen anyone arguing against that, but then again I haven't read the whole internet yet.

The sheer volume of information is a modern-day disaster for a lot of mums, as the sea of conflicting advice threatens to drag you to the very bottom of the pit of despair.

So you don't waste precious hours doing all the research for yourself, I've put together a handy summary for you. You're welcome:

- Ensure children have a solid sleep routine or they'll become stunted pork chops who'll never make it past kindergarten but definitely don't sleep-train them or they'll become sociopaths who'll never be able to establish a human connection.
- Allow your children the freedom to explore and challenge themselves without hovering over them but if they get hurt, you ought to have them removed from your care, you neglectful ringpiece.
- Make sure your children get plenty of fresh air and sunshine but don't let the sun actually touch their skin because DO YOU WANT YOUR CHILDREN TO DIE?
- Go back to work to show your kids the value of employment but don't put your kids in day care because why would you have them just so someone else can raise them?
- Allow your children to learn through play because rote learning is harmful to their development but also make sure they know the alphabet, all their numbers, the periodic table and the full text of the UN Charter before they start school.
- Children must eat vegetables, or they'll get scurvy and die, but you mustn't force-feed them or make mealtimes a battleground. Also, you must not feed them anything with sugar in it but also don't be one of those mums who forces her kids to eat carrots at birthday parties because everyone hates those kids. Lighten up, for god's sake.
- Don't force your children to speak to people because you should respect their autonomy and their right to consent but they also need to say, 'Hello' and 'Please' and 'Thank you' to everyone they meet because manners are essential, you complete failure.

- Cherish every moment because it all goes so fast but don't boast about it because then you're just rubbing it in the faces of people who can't have kids. Support but don't smother, be authoritative but never yell, don't overschedule them but provide ample stimulation, give them all your time but don't spoil them, take this job seriously but just relax, you uptight psychopath.

Got all that? Great.

# 62

# Being a mum is easy

If that was all you had to do.

Just hanging out with your kid all day, playing and laughing and cuddling? Yeah, you might go a bit deranged with boredom eventually, but it wouldn't be that difficult.

The hard work is trying to do *everything else*, everything an adult has to do to live—while also being a mum.

Doing the laundry with a screaming child on your leg. Answering work emails while a toddler climbs up your neck. Cooking dinner with your hysterical baby in a bouncer. Having to care for a child when you're sick. Mopping the floors with a kid who insists on running on them while they're wet.

Kids become extra foul when they want your attention, which is pretty much 24/7. So if you need to achieve ANYTHING else in your day, they're going to make your life difficult. It's just how it is. They give zero forks about the fact you're trying to buy groceries so they can eat. They couldn't give a flying mince pie that you need to clean that bathroom, so they don't die from crawling on that furry floor. They just want you—but being an adult requires you to do stuff, and that means you can't always do what they want when they want it.

It's not a bad thing, mind you. They will eventually need to learn that the world doesn't revolve around them and they might need to wait a few minutes for your full attention, but they won't learn it quickly. And they won't make it fun for you while they do.

Everyone could be a great mum and enjoy their kids if that was the only thing they needed to do. But when you add housework, life admin, shopping and paid work on top of that—your patience will be stretched to snapping point.

# 63

# Men can parent too?

Men might not get a lot of 'loving' in those early days but they will get ALL THE PRAISE.

When you're a woman, people will watch you turn yourself inside out for your child, then nod their heads, smile and mutter something about the joys of motherhood.

But if the father of your child looks sideways at a nappy, people will swoon in delight. He's such a natural! What a bloke! Fancy changing the nappies and everything! #dadgoals

People have such low expectations of fathers that if they show even a passing interest in their own child, they'll be rewarded with adoration and confetti cannons.

Women never get confetti cannons, just in case you were wondering. Please don't expect it.

But men? OH MY GOD, he puts the baby to bed? HOW WONDERFUL HE IS!

Oh, what? You're going out to dinner with your girlfriends? Who will watch the baby? Is Daddy going to BABYSIT?

Babysit his own child? No, mate. He's not being paid. He's being a parent.

Dads are great. We love all the dads! They're so important for our kids and they work so hard to be everything for them. But they don't deserve a Father of the Year nomination for looking after their own kids—no more than mums deserve a prize for doing the same.

Can we stop fawning over them when they calm a crying baby? Can we stop hyperventilating when they give a kid a bath?

Have you ever heard a person say to a bloke who's leaving for a two-week business trip, 'But who will look after the baby?' or 'Gosh, you're lucky you have a wife at home to babysit your child!'

Nope.

When we squeal because a dad has been A DAD, it's a bit like someone gasping in shock and telling a woman they're so impressed she can reverse park. Like OH MY GOD, that's SUPER impressive! Well done you for having spatial awareness skills, you clever clogs!

Well, thanks a bunch, but I'm not a moron, Gary.

Most dads are pretty awesome. They're perfectly capable of looking after their own children ON THEIR OWN. Can we stop acting like they've recently recovered from a head injury and have finally relearnt how to put on socks?

Or, alternatively, if we really can't stop celebrating men who parent their children, can we—at the very least—THROW WOMEN A MOTHER-LOVING PARADE FOR DOING THE SAME THING?

# 64

# The mental load

For a dad, coming home from work is lovely. He's been working hard and he's exhausted so all he wants to do is come home. He might need to bath the baby; he might even put the baby to bed. But being at home seems easier, calmer, than being at work.

Going to work for a mother is lovely. She gets to step away from the housework, the appointments, the whingeing, the cleaning, the admin, the organisation, the cooking, the shopping. She gets to sit down in one spot. She gets to talk to adults, have a hot cup of coffee and use her brain, completing one task at a time. Driving home is a delicious chunk of me-time, and when she walks in the door, her work begins.

Home is a break for men. Work is a break for women.

Why? It's the mental load.

Men are fantastic at focusing on one task at a time. If they're with the baby, they're only with the baby—thinking about the baby, caring for the baby, responding to the baby's needs.

Women aren't so lucky. If a woman is with the baby, she's also looking at the dirty dishes, she's wondering if there's any capsicum for tonight's stir-fry, she's looking at the rash on the baby's leg and wondering if she needs to call the doctor, she's glancing at her phone as a work email pops up and she's also trying to focus on the baby who probably needs to eat more vegetables according to the article she just read on the bus to work this morning. It's not just the way a woman's brain works; it's how we're *trained*, because no one else is volunteering to think about these things.

All the plates are spinning and we're the only ones watching them. And no one is noticing us doing all the watching.

Everything a mother does will be what everyone expects her to do. This means that nothing you do will be valued as special or extraordinary. It's simply your 'job'.

But do you know what people in the workplace value more than money? Acknowledgement. People would willingly accept less pay if they knew the effort they put in each day would be noticed and appreciated by their boss.

That's all mums are asking for: for our mental load to be *seen* and *appreciated*.

\*    \*    \*

Just a short note to let you know that parenting really is a two-person job.

Not always two at a time—although two at a time is sometimes necessary in times of poonamis and vomitgeddons. But ideally, you'll have someone to come in and give you a break now and then. When you've been wrangling an unruly child all day long, you need a break, even if it's just five minutes when the responsibility for your child isn't on *you*.

So what I'm saying is: if you know a single mum, give her all the praise and awards. And, if you are able to, step in and give her a hand now and then to let her know she's not alone.

And if you ARE a single mum, I bow down. You are the strongest of the strong, doing the job of two people and killing it. Even if you think you're not, YOU ARE.

# 65

# Husband rage

There are people out there who think having a baby will 'save the relationship'.

Those people are wrong.

Having a baby *might* make you love your partner even more because watching someone become a parent alongside you can be pretty intoxicating. But this will probably only happen to people who already quite like each other, not couples on the rocks.

It's far more likely that your relationship will become a constant dance of wanting to kill your partner and then not killing him. (No one ever gives a woman credit for not murdering the father of her children in the middle of the night, by the way.) It's not easy.

And this can happen even if everything was fine before the baby arrived.

It can be frightening to feel such rage towards someone who, deep down—really deep down—you truly love. Especially when, just a couple of months ago, you couldn't wait to see this person become a daddy. You dreamed about how your little family would look and you knew everything would be perfect.

And now, in the middle of the night, as you try to feed a screaming baby next to that sleeping hulk of useless nipples and unparalleled sleeping ability, you feel slightly less enamoured.

It's always in the dark of night that you turn to this person and start resenting everything he represents. His ability to fall asleep in seconds. His inability to hear anything at all. His refusal to lie awake and listen to the baby breathe all night like you apparently need to do now because your brain won't let you drift off. His abdominal muscles that are still functional, the control he has over his bladder. His la-di-da lifestyle with lunch breaks and tea breaks and fresh air and ADULT CONVERSATIONS and LIFE. The fact his career is forging ahead without any concern about his commitment to his work now that he's a parent.

It's perfectly normal to look at that snoring lump and dream about gouging out his perfectly un-bloodshot eyeballs and hanging them over the crib like a mobile.

You can blame lack of sleep and raging hormones. When you're so tired you start forgetting words like 'milk' and 'bowl', it's understandable that watching a person sleep could send you into a homicidal rage. It's like starving for three weeks and then watching someone binge on pizza. And you can't exactly rage at the baby, can you?

It'll be okay. Most women go through periods of planning out their partner's death in exquisite detail. Most of us don't follow through.

You'll calm down and start to like them again. Eventually. Usually around the time you decide you want another child.

# 66

# Baby weirdness

Every time your baby goes through a change, you'll start Googling, looking up your baby books and asking all your mum friends, because you simply MUST find a reason for why your baby is being such a toad.

You can tear your hair out trying to find a reason for a sudden change in behaviour. Surely it can't be normal for your baby to be awake every minute of the day/terrified of food/blatantly plotting to murder you?

But sometimes babies are just being *weird*.

The official diagnosis is Baby Weirdness.

Fever? No.

Teething? No.

Sick? No.

Wet nappy? No.

Hungry? No.

Hot or cold? No.

Well, clearly their huffy mood this week is just Baby Weirdness.

You don't need to know all the answers. Sometimes there's no real or tangible explanation for the whingeyness or the clinginess or the sudden predilection for violence.

Actually, there probably is but you're never going to know because they can't say things like, 'You know what, Mum? I am positively enraged at everyone today because it's way too sunny outside and the music you play is pathetic so stop looking at me or I'll stick my foot down your throat until you CHOKE TO DEATH,' or something like that.

Babies get pissed off. They get moody or grumpy or just a bit emo. Just like adults. Funny, that.

# 67

# Babies sleep, right?

The promise of a six week old who sleeps through the night is what keeps some mothers going in those early days.

Shame it's such a scam. Some babies just won't sleep. Ever. No matter what the 'experts' say.

You know who's an expert in sleep? Any parent whose kid doesn't sleep. I haven't slept in six years so I promise I know FAR more about getting a child to sleep than a parent whose kid has been sleeping through from day one. Those people know nothing about sleep.

I mean, I'm happy for them and their smug sleeping babies. But it's nothing they did. You can't teach six week olds anything other than poking out their tongues. They aren't picking up on a 'relaxed vibe'. They're not 'syncing' with their parents' routine. They can't tell time. They just like sleeping.

But me? I know it all. I've read the entire internet back catalogue on sleep.

My son was a sleep-hater from the start. He'd wake eight or nine times a night until I was ready to stab my husband (not my child—he was just a baby—but I needed to take my rage out on someone). We went to sleep school and after four nights the nurses just clucked, 'Oh, he's just a little mystery, isn't he?'

We hired a sleep consultant who taught us a roll-and-pat technique, which worked for a few days until the baby figured us out and any attempt to roll him on his side would result in wild kicking and screaming.

Then one day, when he was about thirteen months old, he slept. And then he did it again. And again, and again, and again. To this day I have no idea what happened. He just decided to give sleep a go. (He no longer sleeps through, btw. But that's a story for another day.)

And then I had my daughter and she slept. Well kiss my self-satisfied arse: I'D WON. I'd figured it out. SO MUCH SKILL. Then, at around twelve months, she forgot. Not sleeping anymore, thanks for coming. Every expert I spoke to couldn't figure it out because she did the one thing they all bang on about: *she put herself to sleep.* She self-settled. THE HOLY GRAIL. Everything is about getting them to put themselves to sleep, right? But no one could tell me how to get her to STAY ASLEEP.

But I tried not to panic because in my time, I've learnt two things: it's not me, and it'll pass. I could tie myself in knots about all the things I've done wrong or I could just wait it out.

Of course, that also means enduring the advice. SO MUCH ADVICE.

I had one new mum tell me the secret to having a sleeper was all down to a good diet. Her kid was six months old and had just started solids. What kind of diet was that kid on? I mean, I started my kids on crack and Coca-Cola. Was that wrong?

People, hear me when I say this: THERE'S NO SECRET. THERE'S NO MAGIC ANSWER. It sucks, and it doesn't help you, but if you're losing your mind tonight just know that you're not alone and it's not your fault.

Every kid is different. They'll sleep when they sleep.

# 68

# Nap-time enemies

Nap-time is a sacred ritual for mothers. It's a time of respite and rejuvenation. It's a time for unsupervised toilet breaks, uninterrupted meals and maybe even a few precious moments in the laundry. What joy! So you can understand the rage and devastation caused when something or someone WAKES THE BABY.

These nap-time enemies are the mortal foes of every parent.

## The transfer

Beautiful baby angel is sound asleep in your arms but now you need to execute The Transfer to move the baby from your arms to the cot. Cirque du Soleil could start a new show based on the contortionist acts performed in nurseries around the world because mothers will turn themselves inside out to do this without waking the baby.

When my son was especially sensitive to movement (and light and sound and the tides and the goddamn gravitational pull of the earth), I would lower him down with my chest still touching his face, so he wouldn't wake from the sudden change of temperature. Sounds reasonable, right? Except I couldn't phys-ically do this with both feet on the floor, so I ended up balanced like a seesaw on the railing of his cot, legs in the air, head pressed into the mattress to stop me suffocating my son. Picture it. It's humiliating.

Don't even get me started on rescuing your arm from under that baby. How many of us have stood there for what felt like HOURS, weighing up the pros and cons of wetting our pants versus waking the baby?

## The creaky knee, clicky elbow, clacky wrist, squeaky shoulder . . .

. . . or any part of your body that betrays you by cracking like buck-shot as you lower your sleeping babe into the cot. It's the ultimate heartbreak when your own body lets you down. It's impossible to avoid and always seems to happen right at the moment you think you've succeeded in The Transfer. Just as you move away from the cot—POW! Cue the tears. (Yours *and* your baby's.)

## Sound/frequency waves?

Or whatever it is that makes you aware that someone is close to you—or someone is moving away. You know how the air sort of changes when someone is in your personal space? That's how babies know when you're walking away from the cot. The only solution is to walk so slowly you feel the earth shifting under your feet. You might make it to the door by the end of the nap.

## The creaky spot on the floorboards

That frigging creaky spot must be avoided at all costs. If necessary, you'll turn yourself into Spiderman and climb the walls to get around it. I swear I levitated once.

## The bedroom door

The worst tragedy of all is getting the baby to sleep, only to wake them as you close the bedroom door. I now have advanced skills in silent door-closing. The bomb squad has nothing on me. I can close a door so gently that the door itself doesn't realise it's closed.

## The doorbell

WHO RINGS THE DOORBELL? Villains, that's who. Evil bastards who wait until you've put the baby down to ring that fecker loud and clear for the whole street to hear. This also applies to all the arseholes who have ever mowed the lawn during nap time. You horrible, spiteful, houseproud pricks.

## The insane cat

My cat (like most) wishes my baby had never been born. That baby stole all of her attention and affection. She wishes him ill, I'm sure of it. She will sit outside his room and, as I open the door, will start wailing like an alley cat on heat. She is a mastermind.

I'm assured there are also some dickhead dogs who've written, 'Bark like a cock-knocker!' in their diaries for the exact minute the baby falls asleep.

# The phone

Do NOT leave your phone on when you're putting the baby down. My phone has been on silent for years. Seriously. I don't even respond when I hear a ringtone anymore because my phone only vibrates. I've learnt my lesson.

# Sunlight

We moved into a brand-new house when our firstborn was four months old. It was a couple of months until we managed to get some blackout blinds installed. In the meantime? Aluminium foil and cardboard boxes. Our house looked like a cross between a meth lab and a home for conspiracy theorists. But when you have a child who will only sleep inside a vacuum of light and sound, you won't mind looking like degenerates.

# Mumness

This one's the hardest of all to defeat. Even if you've used your mad ninja skills to transfer that baby and you've made it out of the room in ear-popping silence and you've avoided the cat and the phone and the doorbell . . . nothing can stop you from getting outside the door and suddenly, irrationally deciding you need to walk back into the lion's den to check your baby is lying on his back. Or that his sleeping bag isn't suffocating him. Or that he's warm and breathing.

Or because, despite fighting for an hour to get that baby to sleep, you suddenly miss him and just want to take a peek. Because, honestly, what's more precious than a sleeping baby?

# 69

# Night-time momster

Dear darling baby of mine,

It's three in the morning and I'm not myself. To be fair, you've dragged me out of bed at 3 a.m., which is officially within the ugly hours of the morning; nothing good ever happens between 2 and 4 a.m.

Sweetie, I can accept a 1.30 a.m. wake-up. At 1.30 in the morning, I can fool myself into thinking I've only just barely laid my head on the pillow so it's no big deal. I still remember what it was like to dance on tables at one in the morning, so I can forgive a 1.30 wake-up.

If you demand to see me at 4 a.m. I can tell myself you've slept through the night but accidentally woke too early. I've probably had four hours of sleep in a row, which is a winning effort for any parent, so 4 a.m., while not ideal, is not the worst.

But 3 a.m.? It's the middle of the night! WHY WON'T YOU LET ME SLEEP?

Little one, I love you more than words can say. My love is at its biggest when you're fast asleep in your bed. Sometimes the love threatens to carry me up the stairs and into your room so I can scoop you up and shower you with kisses.

Let's be honest, I'm not perfect during the day. Mary Poppins I am not, but I think we can agree that I always manage to tread the line of mental stability because, my darling, in the light of day I can see your face. Your sweet, enchanting, adorable face that makes my heart dance and stops me from leaving you out on the nature strip for the council clean-up. Your face saves you. Every. Single. Day.

But the night-time brings the darkness, and in the dark I can't see your face. Your force field of cute is compromised.

During the day your cries pull at my heart and I run to you to offer comfort and cuddles. At night, they sound like the caw of Lucifer.

During the day your head smells of giggles and pinkie promises. At night, when I'm rocking you back to sleep for the second hour in a row, it smells like the decay of my youth.

I'm not proud of the things I've said and done in the middle of the night, and in the morning, when the guilt sets in and I'm begging your forgiveness, I pray you never remember the time I called you a knob or that other time I said you were embarrassing yourself or when I yelled, 'You're UNSTABLE!' in a fit of startling irony.

I'm so sorry, my sweet babe. It's not your fault. Sort of. I mean, if you just STAYED ASLEEP I might start to act more like a human and less like a creature from the underworld.

It's irrational, this anger. I'm thinking of my lost sleep, I'm thinking of all the other babies out there who know how to sleep, I'm thinking of all the things I've done wrong that make you unable to stay asleep. I'm thinking how every scream is a testament to my failure as a mother. I'm also thinking, deep down inside, how hideous I am for not being more comforting or nurturing.

My heart is telling me to calm down. My brain is telling me that growling at you in the dark certainly isn't helping.

*Please, my baby, forgive me. When my shushing sounds like hissing and my lullabies sound like death metal, I know not what I do. It's not me: it's the night-time momster. I'll try harder. Or, of course, you could always call for Daddy . . .*

*Love Mummy xxx*

# 70

# The night shift

In the cold, hard night, it's easy to feel like you're the only one.

When the world is so quiet you can hear the stars talk, the isolation can be suffocating.

But here's the thing . . .

The night shift is like a secret society for mums. When it's dark and eerie and you're sitting up with your babe, just stop. Be still. Listen. Listen harder . . . can you hear us? The rest of us, sitting up in silence, listening out for you? Welcome to the club, lady.

You can't see, but we're here. Some of us are falling asleep while feeding in bed; some of us are scrolling on our phones, trying to stay awake; some of us are hunched over cots, patting bottoms and shush-shush-shushing with increasing levels of aggression and trying to remind ourselves that we don't hate the baby. Some of us are losing our mother-loving minds.

But we are all here, right alongside you, looking at that same night sky, wishing someone else knew how we felt.

All of us are doing the thankless night shift, and, like you, we'll be back up again in the morning for the day shift. Because we are mums. And mums DO.

Welcome to the club.

# 71

# Kids' activities are boring

A good portion of any mother's day is spent thinking of things to do to pass the time.

Eventually babies tire of looking at the sky while you perform your Oscar-worthy 'Look! Clouds!' soliloquy. It's time to find something else to occupy their time because it's still nine hours until Daddy comes home and you're already sobbing into your Milo and dreaming of going to the toilet without someone sitting on your lap.

Kids need entertainment. All the bloody time.

Now, let's be clear: newborns do *not* need to be entertained. Your face is entertainment. Hearing your voice is entertainment. Looking at leaves on the trees is entertainment. Looking at leaves is so entertaining they'll probably have a good scream to let off steam and fall into a fitful sleep afterwards.

But after a few months, when your kid can finally look at you straight on without going cross-eyed, you're going to want to find things to fill their non-napping time.

Your *child* is not boring, but spending time doing their activities will make you want to cry a little bit. You'll have the occasional flashback to those days you used to . . . actually, you won't even be able to remember what you did before the baby arrived. It'll seem unfathomable that you ever had a full sixteen hours every day to just do things you wanted to do. What did you even do?

Whatever it was, it was probably more stimulating than banging a ball on a table. Or flipping through the same board book for the seventy-sixth time in an hour.

You might even be tempted to hop on to Pinterest and look up 'sensory activities for six month olds' and I won't stop you. The search alone will eat up a good hour or two of your day. But then you'll realise you don't have a ready supply of pom-poms, water beads and red beans and you'll give up. Or maybe you'll spend four hours packing yourself and your child up, jump in the car to go and buy all the supplies, come home and set it all up; your child will stick his hand in those beans for two and a half minutes and then vomit and playtime will be over for the day.

Sometimes, the mere process of planning and setting up and *almost* executing 'sensory playtime' will make you feel like you've achieved something. A bit like when you used to complete tasks at work. Remember that? When you felt productive? Good times.

The secret is that kids don't want sensory play or educational toys. They want objects that serve as physical barriers, which can be climbed over to get to the things they really want: anything breakable, poisonous or dangerous in your home.

Kids love knives. And fire. And dog poo. And heights. I'm not sure they actually want to stay alive.

# 72

# The harshest critics

It doesn't help when babies are as judgemental as they are demanding. They don't even need to talk to let you know just how disappointing you are. Through a series of screams, slaps, filthy looks and complete indifference, you know exactly what they're saying.

BABY     Sing me a song.

ME       *You are my sunshine, my only . . .*

BABY     STOP. Don't you mothers know any other songs?

ME       *Twinkle, twinkle . . .*

BABY     DON'T YOU DARE. Sing me a real song.

ME       *It was a clear black night . . .*

BABY     I swear to god, if you sing 'Regulate' one more time . . .

ME       What's wrong with 'Regulate'?

BABY     You're impressing no one with the fact you know all the words. It just makes you old and I am embarrassed for you. Sing something more current.

| | |
|---|---|
| ME | *I came in like a wrecking ball . . .* |
| BABY | I can't even look at you. |
| ME | Let's do something else. Let's sit on the floor and play with toys. |
| BABY | Yes! Give me all the toys! |
| ME | Here's a plastic ring with fake keys! |
| BABY | MORE! |
| ME | Here's a plastic monkey! |
| BABY | MOOOORE! |
| ME | Here's a rattle thingy! |
| BABY | WHY DON'T YOU UNDERSTAND? GIVE IT ALL TO ME! |
| ME | Maybe if you stopped throwing them at me you could build your collection. |
| BABY | Stop giving me useless advice and give me more toys. |
| ME | I've given you all the toys. |
| BABY | I refuse to believe you. |
| ME | I literally have no more toys to give you. |
| BABY | You lie through your teeth. I need all my brother's toys. |
| ME | Well, they are *his* toys and you are too little. |
| BABY | Right, so the gender division starts early with you, does it? Already placing limits on me? How do you know I won't absolutely kill it with his Hot Wheels? |
| ME | Please don't do this. |
| BABY | Something is very wrong with you. Please leave. |
| ME | I love you? |
| BABY | I SAID GOOD DAY. |

It could be just me, but I think angry babies are hilarious. The pent-up rage is palpable. How can someone so small have so much fury? Why so irate, little one? Because I tried to give you a toy you didn't want?

Hot tip: they don't often like it when you laugh at their anger. Which kind of makes it funnier. It's a vicious, hilarious circle.

The best part is, they get over their rage as quickly as it hits. They have no commitment to their anger whatsoever. Point at a picture of a dog and they'll go from hissing to giggling in two seconds flat. If only adults were so easily pleased.

# 73

# Maternity leave goals

When you were pregnant and staring down the barrel of months and months off work, you might have dreamed about all the things you'd get done in that time.

You'd finally learn a new language.

You'd learn the piano like you've always wanted to.

You'd tear through all those books on the shelf, then you'd organise that cupboard. You'd scrapbook every milestone in the baby book. It'd be such a time of learning and growth for you and your new baby.

Your baby, of course, would come along for the ride. She'd play on the floor during your piano lessons. You'd read to her in Spanish because then she'd learn it too. She'd be such a hit at your French cookery classes and the other students would fight to cuddle her. Ahh, the delicious promise of all That. Free. Time.

I'm sorry, but it might not quite work out that way. In fact, it's pretty easy to spend the twelve whole months of maternity leave *trying* to start something and twelve whole months never finishing anything.

It's not that babies create so much havoc you can't breathe; it's simply a matter of priorities. During this first year, your priorities will shift so much you'll laugh at the things you thought you'd want to do.

Babies do take up a lot of your time. Realistically, your days will be filled with playing with the baby, cleaning the baby, feeding the baby, trying to get the baby dressed and out of the front door, getting the baby to sleep and taking photos of the baby. That doesn't sound like much, but it'll fill every spare minute of your day.

You might, if you're lucky, get about two hours in the day free while the baby naps. Two hours, you say? Plenty of time to learn how to crochet!

Absolutely—just as soon as you tidy up all the toys, clean the kitchen and the food-covered floor, run a load of laundry, eat some lunch and sit down for four minutes with your eyes closed so you can catch up on the six hours of sleep you didn't get last night.

And then she wakes from her nap.

Having goals is great. Have lots of goals. But don't be hard on yourself if you don't manage to write your first book during your maternity leave. Keeping a baby fed, entertained, clean and happy is a full-time job, and don't let anyone tell you otherwise.

Taking five minutes in the day to sit and relax isn't a crime either. If it makes you feel recharged and re-energised, then that's what you need to do to keep going. And if you do pick up a few words of Spanish, then well bloody done, you.

# 74

# Let's get physical

There's a reason women can't have children in their old age: mums need to be fit. Motherhood is a surprisingly physical job. Men can have babies well into their eighties and nineties because back in the cavemen days, blokes didn't do any of the raising of children. All they needed to do was the fertilising. It's the women who needed to do everything else.

You can't half-arse this job. It's Aerobics Mum Style from day one. Here's the timetable.

## Flexibility

My children now share a room and they cannot fall asleep without me touching them. I don't have to rock or pat anymore but I must be touching their bodies. Their beds are on opposite sides of the room. So that's fun.

You'll also get a work-out in the car, trying to reach dropped toys from the driver's seat. There are also the many hours you have to sit on the floor to play with stupid trains, and the dance classes that require you to get involved and touch your toes like the two year olds next to you.

## Core

You'll perform contortions trying to put your sleeping baby down in her cot without waking her. You'll also be familiar with the ninja drop-and-roll, accompanied by the commando crawl. Once you reach a higher level in your core strength you'll find you can almost defy gravity as you attempt to leave your child's room without making a sound.

## Weights

Women carry bags with purses and phones in them. Mums carry a portable nursery wherever they go. You could set up a campsite with the gear you now carry. You might only have two children but you seem to have 26 litres of water, 8 apples and 17 books in your bag at any given moment. Frequently you will be lugging 72 bags as well as multiple children in your arms.

This is the reason you are shrinking, btw. Your bones are compressing from the sheer weight of the garbage you carry every day.

## Cardio

Every afternoon at 4 p.m. you will commence a three-hour non-stop HIIT circuit. You will not take a break until your children are in bed. It will involve: lifting children, running after children, picking up after children, washing children and—the most intense station of all—putting pyjamas on children. It's a punish.

## Endurance

You will spend hours trying to sit down. Every time you think this is finally it, and your bum hits the seat, BAM. He needs a drink, or a snack. She falls and hurts herself. He decides he wants a completely different activity. She does a poo. He starts to dismantle your house. You'll realise you should probably hang out that washing . . . it never ends. You're on your feet all day long.

The greatest tragedy is that despite all of this cardio and weight training, you don't seem to lose any weight or build any muscle. Surely you should have killer biceps by now?

# 75

# Warning: bad for your health

They're tiny but they're mighty. Mighty dangerous. And for miniature people, they pack a punch.

I mean they'll injure you in their daily business of being out-of-control, self-involved, completely nonplussed humans who'll headbutt you in the eye socket and laugh about it.

A cosy cuddle while reading a book will almost always end with a head-to-chin collision, often causing teeth-through-tongue syndrome.

Popping on a child's T-shirt will almost always result in that child's fingers inside your eyeballs or their forehead connecting with your nose.

Picking up a screaming child is a dangerous activity with the high probability of an eye-socket fracture when the child performs the impressive suddenly-upside-down move and you get a heel straight in the face.

Sitting down to play trains will feel innocent enough, until a Thomas takes flight and your mouth stops its trajectory, leaving you with a fat lip you need to explain away at day care drop-off.

A child who wants to climb up on the couch to cuddle you is a child who is 100 per cent going to stick a knee or elbow straight into your boob or thigh, which is exponentially more painful than you'd think.

You'll be standing in the kitchen, innocently making lunch, and a child will walk over and stand with their rubber-soled torture boots on the very tops of your bare feet so it feels like the flesh will tear right off the bone.

Men don't have much to fear in this world but if they're just going to stand around like masters of their domain, they should expect sudden, unprovoked headbutts to the ball sack. (Hate to say it, but it wouldn't have happened if he'd worn safer clothes. Totally asking for it.)

My child once screamed until I agreed to reach for the water bottle which had fallen on to the floor of the car. At the lights, I reached over to get that bloody water bottle and punched myself in the chest with the gear stick. Broke my ribs. She didn't even touch me but it was still all her fault and I won't hear otherwise.

Babies should come with a health warning.

This child:

- will ruin your body, your hair and your face and may leave you with a pelvic floor that has the willpower of Augustus Gloop
- will keep you awake for months on end and when they finally sleep—you won't be able to anymore
- will cause fear-based hallucinations where you vividly imagine their demise any time they're within 500 metres of a dangerous object

- will ruin your back with the constant carrying and picking-up of things off the floor
- will hike your blood pressure to dangerous levels with the simple refusal of food
- will reduce you to a diet of rejected toast crusts and banana ends
- will render you incapable of watching sad stories on the news without catastrophic eye leakage
- will steal all of your time and all of your money.

And despite all of this, you will love that child more than anything you've ever loved and just as you start to see straight again, you'll turn around and say you want another.

Lucky they're so damn cute.

# 76

# The laws of motherhood

Kids are great, until they're not.

This is important. Remember it.

Every child is like a fingerprint; none are perfect. Or if they are perfect, they won't stay that way for long.

Something you need to know about kids is: the minute you sing their praises, they will undergo a complete personality refurbishment and you will regret the day you ever opened your mouth.

This message is particularly important for anyone prone to feeling smug or superior about their parenting skills. Kids have a very special superpower, and that is to make an idiot out of you the *minute* you mention how wonderful you are at this motherhood gig.

This is one of the basic laws of motherhood.

The moment you boast about how successfully you've trained your child to sleep is the moment your child goes through a sleep regression that lasts months.

Your eye-roll at your sister-in-law's inability to get her child to eat anything other than plain pasta is a signal for your child to start refusing any food with colour. Welcome to The Beige Diet.

Your humble brag to your girlfriends about your child's expanding vocabulary and knowledge of all the colours will perfectly coincide with your child's wobbling steps over to the crusted bin lid where he will stare you straight in the eye as he sticks out his tongue and takes a big long lick.

What I'm saying is, when things are going well, it's best to keep it to yourself. Don't even mention it to your partner. A knowing look could be enough to bring it all crashing down. Don't say I didn't warn you.

There are some other laws of motherhood. They're much like Murphy's Law, but for mums.

1.  Anything that can go wrong *will go wrong.*
2.  The more desperately you need your child to nap, the more strenuously he will refuse to nap—yet the day you need to leave your home at a certain time, he will sleep like the dead.
3.  As you carry your gravely ill child into the doctor's office, she will undergo a miraculous recovery.
4.  The more expensive and educational the toy, the more your child will hate it.
5.  The amount of love and attention you put into making a meal for your child is directly proportional to the athleticism he will display as he throws it across the room.
6.  The quieter the child, the more permanent the damage she is causing.
7.  Your child will wet himself exactly two minutes after he promises he doesn't need to go potty.
8.  The more excitement and planning involved in a rare girls' night out, the more vigorously your child will start spewing the hour before your departure.

9. The more exhausted you are, the more enthusiastically your child will tap-dance on your last nerve.
10. Your child will want nothing to do with a toy until another child touches it.
11. Your child will receive a self-inflicted black eye, fat lip or ragged-nail scratch to the face the day before a big event where many family photos will be taken.
12. The exact thing you don't want your child to say will become her favourite phrase.
13. In a room the size of Narnia, the only place your child will find to sit is on you.
14. The first night your child sleeps through the night, you will suffer an attack of insomnia.
15. Your children will happily entertain themselves until you step into the shower.
16. The satisfaction you feel after cleaning a room is directly proportional to the speed with which your child will appear at the door to destroy it.
17. The more you treasure that sweet outfit your child is wearing, the more permanent the stains she'll inflict upon it.
18. Your child will refuse water all day but bedtime will bring a thirst no water can quench.
19. The more deadly/dangerous/poisonous the item, the more quickly your child will locate it and/or put it in her mouth.
20. Your child will pour a full bottle of water over himself on the day you don't pack a change of clothes.

# 77

# The world versus mothers

Babyhood is often when you begin to fully realise just how hard motherhood is. It's not your child, mind you. You love your child with all your heart. But it is possible (and normal) to love your child with a fierceness that scares you, while also resenting some aspects of motherhood.

There's the shame of being dismissed as 'just a mum', even though you're highly qualified in your chosen career—from the moment you become a mother, you are no longer 'Amanda, CEO', you're 'Amanda, mother of one'. There's the injustice of being side-lined in your job, even though you're far more efficient than anyone in your team. You've heard the praise heaped on men for doing the bare minimum as fathers, even though the lioness's share of the work falls to you. You finally see all the ways society judges women, no matter what decisions they make, because being a mum is often a lose–lose situation.

Take your children out and you're annoying everyone. Keep them home and you're starving them of life experience. If you formula-feed, you're poisoning your child. If you breastfeed, you should do it far, far away where no one has to see it happen, and you definitely should be stopping by that child's first birthday otherwise you're a sicko. If you discipline your child, you're evil. If you don't, you're spoiling them. Literally anything you do, someone will have an issue with it.

They will tell you that you always need to put your children first. You need to value their happiness above your own. You need to sacrifice all the things that make you YOU, or you're selfish. You shouldn't even want to wear make-up or get your hair done. Why would you? That would take time away from your child. You need to cherish every moment of hardship, sacrifice and martyrdom.

If you show a hint of unhappiness, regret, bitterness, frustration, annoyance or selfishness, you are a *bad mother*.

Well, welcome to the bad mum club, sister. It's not overly exclusive here. It's basically an open-door policy because literally every single person to ever raise a child is here too.

There are a couple of things that'll really get the judgement pumping:

## Staying at home or going back to work

Mothers who go back to work are neglecting their children. Why have kids if you're just going to hand them to someone else to raise? It's selfish to put your own needs first.

Mothers who stay at home have given up their brains to sit and play with fingerpaints and watch TV. They're not contributing anything to society so there's no need to engage them in conversation.

Mothers who go back part-time can't be taken seriously in the workplace because they're only half-willing to commit to their careers but they're also handing their kids over to strangers some of the time, so WHAT A PIECE OF WORK SHE IS.

These attitudes are everywhere and the injustice will make you boil.

Let's be clear:

If you're working because you HAVE to and you'd prefer not to starve your children, or live on the streets, good on you. You are providing. You've made the right decision for your family.

If you're working because you LIKE work and you ENJOY feeling productive, good on you. You're allowed to live your life while also being a mum. You're setting a great example for your kids. You've made the right decision for your family.

If you're staying at home because that's what works best for your family, good on you. You've made sacrifices, and being at home with young kids is a seriously tough and draining job. You've made the right decision for your family.

If you're studying or working part-time or working from home or volunteering or trying to fit eighteen different casual jobs in around three different types of care for your kids, good on you. YOU'VE MADE THE RIGHT DECISION FOR YOUR FAMILY.

Trying to achieve ANYTHING while raising kids takes effort, organisation, sacrifice, hard work and plenty of love.

NO ONE has it easy. NO ONE has everything just the way they want it. EVERYONE sacrifices in one area or another and NO ONE feels like they're giving enough to every area of their life.

And, it has to be said, handing your child to a stranger to look after is one of the hardest things a mother does. You thought you'd skip off with a smile on your face but now you're sitting in the car park, crying your eyes out and craning your neck to see if you can catch a glimpse of your baby who is probably being neglected by those total strangers you just dumped him with. What were you thinking? That you could just discard your child and go and have a career like the selfish wildebeest you are? You need to march back in there and snatch your baby up before they corrupt him with their wanton carelessness.

All this time you thought you'd enjoy being away from this child who has worn you down with his need, and now that day is here, you've realised he's a part of you and you don't even know how to function without him next to you.

## Spending time apart from your child

Women who devote every spare minute to their children are looked at with suspicion and whispers of brain damage—but women who dare to carve out a few minutes away from their children? Selfish, ungrateful beasts.

Motherhood is, allegedly, an exercise in martyrdom. Wanting some time to yourself is viewed as the ultimate betrayal of your children. Doing something that only benefits yourself is a *clear indication* you do not love your child.

The elusive 'me-time' becomes something women talk about in hushed tones like they're talking about cocaine and not just a cup of tea in the backyard with a Kmart catalogue.

People, hear me: *everyone* enjoys spending time away from their children. If they say they don't, they're lying or they're emotionally unhinged. You've got to miss your kids now and then. It's human to want to be free of responsibility occasionally. You *can* have a few hours apart without permanently damaging your baby's psyche.

The great injustice is, even if you do manage to spend some time away from your kids, it won't be the same as it was before, because a part of you will always be pulling you back to them. Time away will always be tainted with worries about how they're coping without you, and, most annoying of all, you'll just miss their cute little heads.

The only way to be a real winner in your new life as a mum is to not give a dirty sheet what anyone else thinks about you and how you choose to live your life. You do you, boo.

# 78

# Opinions and advice: part 3

If you make the mistake of saying, out loud, *anything* that suggests you're struggling with your baby, you'll be met with feverish grins, spewing unsolicited advice that always starts with, 'Have you tried . . . ?' in a way that suggests you couldn't possibly have tried the most basic of suggestions because you're clearly a moron.

'My baby refuses to take the bottle.'

'Have you tried using a different type of bottle?'

'Why no, Julia, I didn't think of that at all! I've been forcing the same teat in his mouth for weeks hoping he'd suddenly learn to love it. I haven't spent $600 on every bottle on the market at all!'

'My child refuses to eat anything green.'

'Have you tried telling him that you won't be making anything else for him? I find you need to be really strict and not offer other foods because they can be so manipulative.'

'Excellent advice, Becca. Thanks so much! I mean, my child is seven months old and doesn't understand where I go when he can't see me but I'm sure he'll be able to understand the concept of starving if he doesn't eat what I've made for him right now.'

'My baby struggles to fall asleep unless I'm holding him.'

'Have you tried patting / shushing / singing / humming / white noise / interpretive dance / just walking out?'

'Yeah, yeah, Jennifer, I have. I have tried all of those things, because I also have access to Google and I can read. But thanks for making me feel like I must know absolutely nothing.'

Of course we know people mostly mean well, but we also know that if they had any sort of confidence in our skills, they wouldn't offer up such basic suggestions, because surely they'd know we've tried everything? Absolutely *everything*.

# 79

# When your baby is sick

Nothing can prepare you for the fear, panic and desperation you will feel when your child is sick. Calling an ambulance or racing to the emergency room is a mixture of sheer terror and unwavering focus. You have a job and that's getting your child well—and nothing will stop you.

One of the hardest things you'll ever do is hand your child to someone else for help. There's no question you'll do it; you'd ask your mortal enemy for help if it would protect your child. But handing them over means you're trusting someone else to love and care for them like you would. That's a big gamble to take. Letting go of control means having faith—too much faith to ask of any mother.

Watching your child struggle to breathe or wailing in pain, or seeing them groggy and lethargic, you're reminded that this child of yours isn't a guarantee. This big beautiful love, the bright future you've planned, the person you want them to be . . . none of that is certain. Every day of your life is about trying to get to that future but when they're sick, you're reminded that no one can promise they'll be there.

You finally realise how much you would sacrifice for your child. You would take their place in a heartbeat, you'd take on all the pain without question, you'd climb up on that bed and lay down your life.

But then again, the thought of *you* dying can be just as terrifying.

*My baby,*

*Sometimes I hold you long after you've fallen asleep, cradling your little body next to mine, your head snuggled into my neck, your cheek resting on my chest.*

*And I squeeze you.*

*I squeeze you to bursting and press your heart into mine so my love might burn into your skin like a tattoo. So that if I ever die, you will remember what my love feels like. So, when you've forgotten the sound of my laugh or the curve of my smile or the smell of my skin, you might remember what it felt like to be loved by me.*

*I squeeze you and whisper, 'remember me' because I'm so afraid of leaving you. And I tell you I love you because there are no bigger words to describe it even though it feels so much greater than plain old love.*

*You don't know what I'm doing and if you were awake you'd just push me away and run off to play. But I want you to know that I do this. I want you to know how much you mean to my life and how completely you've stolen my heart. I want you to know that if I ever left, I would be right there, inside your heart, because you're not just some person I love— you are a part of my soul. I could never fully leave you behind.*

*I can't bear to think about not being there to hold you when you cry or to explain where I've gone. The thought of you calling for me at night rips at my heart. I never want you to feel that pain. In a perfect world, I will always be by your side so you'll never need to know what life is like without me cheering you on.*

*Darling, you are crazy and wild and so full of joy it makes my world spin off-kilter. I can't wait to spend the rest of my life with you. I hope that's a really, really long time.*

*Love Mummy xxx*

# 80

# This sucks

Never before have parenting skills been under more scrutiny than they are today. Every photo we post on social media is analysed for clues of poor mothering, and every status update is criticised for not being more #grateful #blessed. People have no tolerance for a whingeing mother.

Hating the tantrums doesn't make us hate our kids. Wishing our kids would just listen for one minute doesn't make us regret our family. Praying for a moment of solitude doesn't mean we'd ever want to go back to our life before having children.

But being able to say, 'This sucks!' is *vital* because sometimes parenting is sucky and we need to be able to say it out loud or we might implode under the pressure of being so goddamn #grateful all the time.

A new mum is flooded with images of what motherhood 'should look like'. A scroll through Instagram will show her a variety of picture-perfect families:

- the mum of a two week old who's just whipped up a healthy batch of cookies
- the six month old sitting in a silk suit his mother has just spent an hour ironing
- the first birthday party styled by professional party planners.

What about the mum who still can't walk two weeks after giving birth? Or the mum who can't get her child to sit still long enough to dress her in fancy clothes? And the family who can only afford a cake from Woolies with an old candle stuck in the top? A mum who's not allowed to talk about the hard times is a mum who feels alone.

It can be so isolating scrolling through Facebook or Instagram and thinking, 'I haven't done *any* of this. I'm a failure.'

You're not a failure. You're *so* normal. But we don't see 'normal'. All we see is the small minority who are killing it—or *pretending* to kill it for likes.

The women behind these accounts don't mean any harm, but they don't realise the damage they're causing vulnerable new mums whose lives look nothing like that perfectly styled vignette that took an hour to set up and photograph. It can make some new mums feel like losers because their lives don't look like that and their kids don't act like that and they can't afford houses like that. It can lead to some really self-destructive thoughts and actions. People will spend money they don't have trying to dress their children in bespoke linen rompers and handcrafted leather moccasins when really, kids are perfectly happy in the $3 Kmart shorts they can run around in and get dirty in, because linen rompers are uncomfortable and a bitch to keep clean.

A quick glance behind the scenes would tell you that no one's life is perfect. Just outside the frame of that Pinterest-worthy playroom photo is a pile of plastic junk pushed into the corner.

Moments before that sweet photo of a chubby toddler was taken, that kid pulled her mum's hair as she forced that broderie dress over her head. The photo of that sleeping angel was taken during the four whole minutes he slept that day, in between bouts of screaming and wailing. But that's not shareable content, is it?

I wish more of those picture-perfect mums could realise that while it's lovely to be admired for your perfect life, nothing compares to the comfort of other mums when you admit you don't love every moment of your day. Having friends and teammates to laugh and cry with will fill your heart and soul ten times more than having fans who admire you from afar. I can't imagine how isolating it must be for someone who's having a hard time but can't admit it in case everyone sees it's all a façade.

All mums need to vent now and then because that's how we discover we're not alone. Being told you're perfect must be nice, but you know what feels better than a pat on the back? The embrace of support. Telling people you're falling and feeling their arms catch you before you hit the ground.

Parenthood has some dark days but getting through it is easier when you're able to say, 'This sucks', and having people around you saying, 'Yeah, sometimes it really does.'

# Part four
# The toddler years

or

*How is this my life?*

*Dear mum, mum, mum, mum, mummy, muuummmyyy, muuuuuuuuuum, mummy, mum,*

*A day with a toddler is like walking through the most beautiful, enchanting meadow you've ever seen, sprinkled with daisies, showered with sunshine. As you wander through this world of unparalleled beauty, you see, out of the corner of your eye, a giant quokka on a skateboard, because why not? Toddlers never make sense. But you find yourself feeling a tiny bit anxious: this day feels too lovely to be real.*

*And then, without warning, you step on a landmine and lose your left leg.*

*Toddlers are the most delicious little people—hilarious, adorable, heart-burstingly precious and sweet. But nothing good is ever free.*

*You'll love watching them learn to talk, then wish they knew how to be quiet.*

*You'll be so proud of how independent they're becoming, then explode when they insist on doing things 'myself'.*

*You'll melt with the constant cuddles and 'I love you's, then be blindsided by their cold-bloodedness.*

*You'll be filled with joy as you witness them learning about the world around them, then wish they weren't quite so observant with your bad habits.*

*You'll marvel at how quickly they grow into real people, and you'll be worn down, every day, with how illogical and irrational they are.*

*Welcome to the magical mystery ride of toddlerhood, where logic is dead and pants are optional.*

*With every day that passes, your child is moving away from you. The baby that barely left your side now has her own agenda, and you are just an observer and guide. Suddenly, feeding, cleaning and entertaining your child aren't enough. Now you need to try and make sure she doesn't become a menace to society. And she won't make it easy on you.*

*Because there's a change that comes sometime after the first birthday when a child realises you don't have supernatural powers and you can't actually compel them to do anything.*

*One day you'll look over and see your toddler about to do something he shouldn't. You'll say, 'NO' in your very best mum voice, and your darling little babe will look you straight in the eye with a smirk that says, 'Oh yeah? And what are you going to do about it?'—and he'll go right ahead and do it. With a smile.*

*It's a shift in power that signals the beginning of the end. The toddler years have begun. So mount up, mofo. You gave birth to this tiny psychopath—you've only got yourself to blame.*

*Toddlerhood is when you truly become a mum. If you survive this, you can survive anything. And you will survive. Probably. If your child allows it.*

*Love Lauren xx*

*PS: Yeah, you still don't know what you're doing. FYI.*

# 81

# Toddlers are the worst

The fact that we allow toddlers to grow into pre-schoolers is proof of the unconditional love of a parent.

Honestly, if you knew an adult who acted like a toddler, you'd probably get some sort of court-ordered protection to keep them away. They're insane, inappropriate, totally unreasonable and often violent. You would never accept any of this from anyone else. But from a toddler, we let it slide.

Let's have a look at some of the standard behaviours of toddlers as performed by a group of 52 year olds:

- You and Barb are going shopping. Barb would like to go shopping in the nude. You look at Barb, boobs hanging to her waist and explain that we all need to wear clothes to the shops. She kicks you in the chin and runs away.

- Gary is hopping into the car for a 10.15 a.m. appointment. It's now 10.13 a.m. and you have spent the last 45 minutes explaining that you really need to go because you're going to be late. Gary opens the door and, despite his bad hip, manages to swing his whole body into the boot of the car in an effort to escape you. When he finally gets into his seat he assumes the two-by-four position and refuses to bend in the middle so you end up karate-chopping him in the beer gut in an effort to do up his seatbelt. As you finally click him in, he knees you in the stomach.

- Ian doesn't like the meal you've made. He stands up, hitches his belt to his nipples, and flicks the whole plate straight at your face.

- Denise is exhausted after a ten-hour shift at work, but instead of going to bed, she's going to stand and scream in your face before removing every item from her bedside table with one swift leg swipe, followed by an interpretive dance routine and incoherent singing. Then she kicks you in the ear.

- Graham has his bed in his own room but at night-time he creeps into your room, climbs into your bed, rubs his stubble all over your neck and kicks you in the back. Over and over and over again. For hours at a time.

No matter how many times you try to tell yourself that your child is just two years old and you are an adult who should be able to keep a steady head, it won't make it any easier to deal with your tiny pest. He's a jerk. An a-hole. A turd. A tiny little fecker. A douchebag, nay, a TWOUCHEBAG. And a twouchebag is just the opening act for the main show, which is the THREENAGER.

If a twouchebag is from the Terrible Twos, a Threenager is from the Throwdown Threes, where life is one big brawl. Or perhaps the Threatening Threes, because all you do is issue threats. Or the

Thankless Threes because it's a SLOG. Maybe it's the Thorny Threes, because it's one big prick of a year. It's definitely the Thirsty Threes because you're going to need to drink.

Of course, you'll throw out the old 'But he is my world, and I love him so much!' every ten minutes or so, to remind everyone you're not complaining, and you're eternally #grateful even when you've just slammed the car door and screamed at the closed window, 'WHY IS THIS MY LIFE?'

But you don't have to do that. We know you love your child. That's never been in question. But, darl, sometimes it's *impossible* to like them.

# 82

# Yes, even your kid

I hate to break it to you. I'd love to give you some hope, but I think it's healthier to be realistic about it.

Your child won't be different. You know those kids running around the restaurant, having tantrums in the supermarket, whingeing about lollies at the check-out? Your child will do that too. You tell yourself your child won't be like that, that you'll teach her how to behave better. But she'll be just like all the other kids.

Because that's how kids behave. All of them. Well, almost all of them. There are, of course, exceptions—a handful of them who break the mould. Congratulations if you get one of them; I'm truly happy for you.

But you probably won't.

Kids aren't like adults (shock!). They don't react to things the way adults do because they haven't had a lifetime of learning the acceptable way to deal with things. So when they want something, they just don't understand why they can't have it right now, and they have no concept of why they should be quiet about it.

Mums have far more patience than normal people. We simply have to. But when you've had 84 minutes of sleep, have only eaten three Vegemite crusts in the past six hours, have a cracking headache and have a trolley load of groceries to buy, your grasp on civility can falter.

It's okay. You're okay. Every mother has had a moment where she'd like to crawl inside the apple display and have a little nap while her child screams about pushing the trolley. You're not a bad mother and you haven't failed.

You know what the problem is? You have a child. It's pretty annoying sometimes. But there is every chance your child will grow up to be amazing.

# 83

# And toddlers
# are the best

You could spend the next couple of years fighting with your home-grown terrorist or you could *lean in*, my friend. Lean into the illogical hilarity that is The Toddler.

They're tiny, they're furiously opinionated and their steely-eyed determination to force everyone to bend to their will is utterly hysterical. Smart adults know it's far better to let their toddler think they're in charge. They kind of are, anyway.

A toddler will always tell you the truth, even if it's not what you want to hear—and especially in public, to complete strangers who probably didn't need to be told how fat their bum-bums are. Toddlers simply must give the brutal truth. All the time. Unless you really want them to tell you something they've done (that they shouldn't have done), in which case they will lie straight to your face, like the unapologetic reprobates they are.

A toddler's zest for life is infectious and adults are powerless to resist. Grown men will strap on fairy wings and tiaras, grandparents will slurp that pretend cup of tea, random strangers will answer that imaginary phone your child just handed to them. If a toddler is inviting you to play, who are you to say no?

They forgive so quickly and can go from screaming fury to sheer delight in thirty seconds flat. They don't hold grudges and when they're happy, they're happy with their whole body and it'll often burst out in the form of a dance—a dance so uninhibited and joyful it'll make you wish you had never grown up.

Life is never boring with a toddler. A toddler will wake you up with a poke in the eyeball, spend the day destroying everything she touches, completely ignore every and any attempt you make to stop her, hurl herself down when you innocently ask what she wants for dinner and go to bed when she frigging well feels like it. But it's impossible to stay angry with toddlers because they're dangerously cute and endlessly hilarious.

Toddlers are so much *more* than babies. You can't even comprehend how drastically they've changed since the day you brought them home. They're no longer fat little burritos to cuddle and feed. Your baby is now a person and the depth and brilliance of this little brain, with opinions and the words to express them, will— ironically—leave you speechless.

Every single day is a new word, a new trick, a new skill learnt, as they grow before your eyes. And in the middle of all this growing and learning, your baby will become someone who *cares* about you—who genuinely wants to know how you're feeling. Their chubby little fingers will cup your face and their roly-poly thighs will climb into your lap, and they will choose to love you and comfort you. They'll love you more than anyone has ever loved you and you will forgive all the moments of chaos for those pudgy arms around your neck and the words 'Lub yoo Mumma'.

They feel things with the intensity of manic circus clowns, and you're forced to ride the wave with them, buoyed by the unadulterated joy and affection only a toddler can give.

Yeah, they're happy little sods. You would be too if you did whatever the hell you wanted without considering the consequences.

Toddlers: all the perks of a sociopath, none of the stigma. You'll love the hell out of them.

# 84

# Moving children suck

Technically, we call this the toddler stage because our kids start to toddle. Which is a lovely image, isn't it? Like tiny baby penguins waddling about, being adorable and penguiny.

I really hope you get your penguin, babe. You deserve one.

I didn't get penguins. I got rhinos. Rhinos that climbed and jumped from very unsafe heights.

Toddlers have zero sense of self-preservation. It's like they're actively trying to kill themselves, preferably by way of a serious head injury. It's unsettling.

When they're born, baby giraffes fall out of their mothers (a six-foot drop onto their heads, mind you), then hop up on their fresh widdle pins and wobble off like it was no big thing. Within an hour of taking their first gulp of air, they're taking care of business. Most of the animal kingdom is like this: the babies pop out and off they go, conquering life like legends.

Not human babies. Somewhere in the evolutionary process, our babies just gave up on the whole 'will to live' thing. Like: *pfft, Mum'll sort that out for me.*

Mums spend more time than you'd think arguing with small people to LIVE, GODDAMN YOU. Because carrying out the bare necessities of existence is just too hard or annoying for kids.

YOU MUST EAT OR YOU WILL DIE. Yeah-nah. Thanks anyway, Mum.

YOU MUST SLEEP OR YOU WILL DIE. Sounds serious but I'm all good, thanks.

YOU MUST GET DOWN FROM THAT GREAT HEIGHT / STOP PLAYING WITH FIRE / NOT RUN IN FRONT OF CARS OR YOU WILL DIE. Calm down, woman, and WATCH MEEEEEE!

Why do they fight us on this? Why don't they just *know* how to live? Are they trying to screw with us or are they just really dumb? IT SHOULDN'T BE THIS HARD, YOU KAMIKAZE MORON CHILD.

Just breathe, eat, sleep, keep warm, don't kill yourself. OKAY?!?!?!

Of course, any and all of your attempts to save your child's life will result in a tantrum. Probably a long one.

# 85

# Pick up/put down

There will be two scenarios, and only two.

1.  They must be carried all the time. Usually at the most incon-
    venient times like when you're trying to make dinner or do a
    poo. They will not allow any other option.
    *or*
2.  They will not be carried. AT ALL. Usually at times you really want
    to carry them, like when you're crossing a car park or trying to
    walk faster than an asthmatic snail.

Ah, remember when your tiny little wombat couldn't even roll?
Good times.

So you just pick them up and walk, right? They're small and
they don't weigh much and you're bigger and stronger, right?

Wrong.

If a child doesn't want to be carried, they have many ways to avoid it, and all of them will be mortifying for you.

- They'll run. Chasing after a toddler in public is humiliating in the extreme because it's a visual representation of how little control you have. And no matter how hard you try, you'll almost always whimper out a pathetic, 'Stop, *please*!'—which will be completely ignored.
- They'll scream. An ear-shattering scream that tells everyone you're trying to abduct this poor creature. (Hot tip: people won't stop you. Even if your child is screaming 'Let me go, I don't want to go with you!', people won't intervene because most people know toddlers are painful and they'll assume you are the parent. Not excellent for kids actually being abducted, btw.)
- They'll perform The Crashing Helicopter. This is a fun one in which your kid will start flinging out limbs like a helicopter that's lost control and is heading for the trees. You'll see parents brace themselves for injury as they dive in with their chins turned to the side so they don't get kicked in the jaw. Again. A hand will inevitably end up in your hair and a chunk of that hair will be pulled out so when you finally grab hold of your kid and straighten up, you yourself will look like you've just crashed into the shrubbery.
- They'll go boneless. This is an impressively effective technique. As you try to scoop up your little twerp, she'll go completely limp, like a human puddle. Knees will buckle, hips will bend, shoulders will slacken and you won't be able to get a grip on anything. A 12-kilo toddler suddenly feels about 85 kilos and you'll need at least three arms to contain the spreading ooze of their body. You end up squatting and frantically scooping like you've just dropped a whole sack of onions and you'll lose your grip on the child at least once but will probably grab

them before they hit the ground a second time, because mum reflexes. But it'll be awkward AF because no one ever said mum reflexes were graceful.

Either way, it's probably going to end in a tantrum. Probably a loud one.

# 86

# You carry it

While toddlers are *physically* capable of doing many things, includ-ing carrying their own belongings, they are *emotionally* incapable of carrying anything. Not a damn thing.

You'll be loaded up with a nappy bag, eight shopping bags, a pair of discarded toddler shoes, a drink bottle and a raggedy bunny rabbit and your toddler will find a special rock (i.e. a piece of gravel) and they'll need you to carry it for them.

In many ways, they're simply cleverer than we are. They've learnt that carrying things is arduous, and you seem able and willing, so why would they carry anything?

And when I say anything, I mean *anything*. They won't carry their own snot if they happen to find a piece on the end of their finger. No, it doesn't matter that they themselves removed it from their own nostril. If it is on their hand and they don't want it there, you will need to take that snot from them. Yes, in the middle of the shopping centre, your child will hold out a finger with a huge booger on the end and you will take that booger off them.

Because this is who you are now. You carry your child's snot. And refusal to carry the snot will result in a tantrum. Probably a violent one.

# 87

# Reality is boring

You will happily become a slave to your child's imagination.

That dolly is real, okay? And that dolly's nappy needs changing right now so you need to get those wipes asap. That spacesuit is her prized possession and how dare you suggest she take it off to go to the shops. That stick he found is very precious and you must hold it carefully because SHHH, DON'T WAKE IT UP!

There is something liberating about walking around the supermarket with a tiny Superman next to you. You're admitting to the world that your toddler is in charge and you don't even care. It's adorable and you know you'll cry when he finally tells you he doesn't need his cape today.

Toddlers let you escape the real world. When you have the choice between eating the 'cupcake' they've made for you in their 'cafe' or worrying about the state of federal politics, the cupcake is the clear winner. The magic they see in every corner makes you realise how desperately boring adulthood is and you'll find yourself becoming more fun, more relaxed, more able to see the sparkle in life. Even if it's for a few minutes, immersing yourself in the bizarre and hilarious world of the toddler feels like a holiday from reality. And you should take as many trips as you can.

# 88

# Silence is deadly

There's this moment when you're sitting down, having a cup of tea and you suddenly realise you haven't heard a sound for a few minutes. Has it been two minutes? Five? Oh god, how long has it been? WHERE IS SHE AND WHAT IS SHE DOING?

You are overcome with *shushpicion*—the unsettling suspicion that hits when things are too quiet.

So you go searching, and you find her. And, like any mother, you have a decision to make. Is the scene you stumble upon serious enough to intervene—and therefore ruin the silence? Or do you let it run its course so you can finish your tea while it's hot? It's a very delicate balance where the cost of the destruction + time required to clean has to exceed the value of tea time.

Let's look at some shushpicious situations and whether intervention is required:

*You see your child pulling out every item from your carefully organised T-shirt drawer. But she's happy and quiet.*

That's an easy one. You let her go. Silent play is priceless; you can deal with the drawer later.

*Your child is calmly and happily painting the carpet with nappy cream.*

You intervene immediately. Silent play might be priceless but that devil cream will never, ever come out.

*You find him sitting in the flowerbed, picking up clumps of mud to rub on his face.*

You might worry he's ruining his clothes, killing the flowers and you simply don't understand his need to rub filth on his face but hey, you're drinking hot tea and he's having the time of his life. Let him go.

*You've gone to visit a friend and her new baby. Your toddler is overly interested in this tiny slug in a wrap and sits staring at the child with intent.*

You'd love to chat with your friend but this is not a time to be hands-off. New mums are notoriously precious about protecting their newborns' safety. And let me tell you now: toddlers never, ever have a newborn's best interests at heart. Never. You don't want your legacy to be: 'Remember that time your kid stuck a rice cracker in my baby's eye?'

*You find your toddler carefully applying your lipstick to his arms.*

Well, this depends on how much you like the lipstick. Because really, you're weighing up the value of the lipstick versus the value of the awesome photo you're going to get at the end of it. Never underestimate the value of a good toddler photo. They'll be treasured for years to come.

Which reminds me: whenever you go to investigate silence, you must ALWAYS take your camera with you. You never know what scene you're about to interrupt and it's considered bad parenting to leave your child teetering on the top of a ladder to go back and get your camera. But if you're there, camera in hand, and they look fairly stable and you don't take your eyes off them, well it's just madness to not take a quick snap before you get them down, isn't it?

P.S interrupting whatever they were doing is going to cause a tantrum. Probably a big one.

# 89

# Nudie rudies

The air on their bodies as they streak out the front door, past the postman and down the driveway, while you run after them screaming 'GET INSIDE NOW!' . . .

This is what toddlers *live* for.

For someone who insists they simply CANNOT put that T-shirt over their head by themselves, a toddler will be surprisingly adept at removing their clothes. Their fine motor skills really come to the fore when they need to be nude. Nude is everything.

So getting UNnude is their idea of a really bad time. Putting clothes on your child, or, as I like to call it, 'putting an octopus into a string bag', will leave you huddled and sobbing in the corner, gazing at the heavens, asking, 'Why have you forsaken me? Please, God, WHY?'

This is how a toddler approaches the daily battle of getting dressed:

## Step 1: Evade

When your mother wants to get you dressed, it's time to evade. By all means necessary. I like your classic Run-and-Hide (in small, impossible-to-reach places). Dodge-and-Weave is another fun one.

Today I tried a simple technique known as The Roll. I lay down on my mum and dad's bed and rolled all over it while she tried to pin me down. Lord alive, it was funny.

I added some super cute whingeing noises just to really set her teeth on edge. I think she caught me smiling once or twice though. I could see her jaw start to clench. Working. A. Treat.

I'd like to highlight this next part to any officers from children's services who might be reading—she practically SAT ON ME to get me dressed. I'm sure this is not an approved parenting technique. If someone could get back to me on that, that'd be great.

To be fair, it was the only way I was leaving the house with pants on, but still, it was not dignified. For her or for me.

## Step 2: Resist

Hear me loud and clear, my friends. YOU DO NOT HAVE TO GET DRESSED AGAINST YOUR WILL. Sure, they may sit on you and forcibly shove your arms into a shirt, but you don't have to just roll over and take it.

FIGHT.

The leg kick is especially damaging to their self-esteem. You've got two legs. They've got two hands, but they need to hold your pants with one hand, so it requires them to try to grasp two legs with the other hand. OH. MY. GOD. It's awesome. It's like watching cats in a boxing ring. 'Uncoordinated' doesn't even begin to describe it.

Today I tried a really great one called The Buck. If you're feeling extra energetic, just jerk your entire body like a raging bull. Olé! That's a good ten minutes wasted.

## Step 3: Destroy

At some point, your parents will need to take their eyes off you to get themselves dressed. This is the perfect opportunity to seek and destroy.

I will leave this one up to you. Freestyle it. You know what you're doing here.

If you really want to make a statement, get yourself undressed.

## Step 4: Throw a tantrum

A long and loud one.

# 90

# All things on the floor

It offends small children deeply when toys, books and clothes are orderly and organised. Their mission in life is to place all their belongings (and any of yours they can reach) on the floor.

The Unpacking Of Things is their raison d'être and 'All things on the floor' is their life's motto. If you own things, they will find those things and they will put them on the floor. Seeing everything you own scattered across a living space makes them feel at peace.

Watching you pack everything away is a weird and fascinating game, and they'll be happy to see you do it, because it gives them another opportunity to unpack all of your belongings again and lay them out for all to see.

They do not know how to put things back, by the way. Even if you showed them 7834 times how to put things back, they would stare at you blankly like you were trying to teach them how to land a plane. And yet, they see you unlock your phone once . . .

As they grow older, they will mix this up with some hide-and-seek. They'll take random items and place them in strange places for you to find. Things like a spatula under your pillow. A football in your shower. A book in your toilet bowl. A headless doll in your bed, which is basically a toddler's way of letting you know they mean business.

My son once took my wedding rings and hid them in a hotel room. We tore that room to pieces searching for them. He was only about fifteen months old and only knew a few words but we interrogated that child like the criminal he was.

He eventually pointed at the room's stereo, where I found my engagement ring inside the cassette deck, and my wedding and eternity bands inside the speaker.

The moral of the story is: cassette decks haven't been used in decades but that doesn't mean you shouldn't check inside every one you see. You have no idea what someone's arsehole toddler might've hidden in there.

PS: Asking them to stop throwing things around the house will result in a tantrum. Probably a throwing one.

# 91

# Kids say the darnedest things

My son's first word was 'cheese'.

He looked at the cheese, he wanted the cheese, he put his hand out and said 'cheese', and I screamed like I'd just won the lotto. Not only was it his first word, it was stupidly cute and, I mean . . . CHEESE. Right? What's not to love about this story?

I don't remember my daughter's first word, because second child (poor little doll). I have a feeling it was 'more', and that sounds like her, so let's just go with that.

First words are magical. After months of whingeing, whining, grunting, pointing and meltdowns because WHY DON'T YOU KNOW WHAT I WANT?, it's a huge milestone when your tiny baby becomes a real human being who has learnt to communicate. Oh, the wonderful conversations you'll have!

First words are written down in books. Videos are taken for posterity. The whole family has agreed they're now called 'hippups' instead of hiccups and the things you wear on your feet are called 'sues'.

The first time your child turns to you and says 'Lub yoo' feels like a windfall after sitting at the same poker machine for two years straight. Oh, how hard you've worked, and it was all worth it for those two tiny words.

Once the words begin, they come thick and fast. One day your child is saying 'cat' and 'ball' and the next day she's saying, 'Can I get a snack please?'

But, like anyone who suddenly discovers a superpower, they soon start to abuse it. Two years of pent-up rage over denied delights and restricted rights comes to the fore.

The mere suggestion of a bath will trigger memories of all those baths given without permission and now your neighbour is at the window, wondering if they should do something about the small child howling, 'NO BATH, DON'T TOUCH ME! LEAVE ME LOOONE!'*

All those times you thought it was okay to swear in front of a six month old haunt you as your child waltzes into day care and sings merrily to her teachers, 'Good morning, bitches!'*

You'll realise you should maybe monitor what your child is watching on TV when he turns to a kid in the playground and says, 'Calm ya tits, son.'*

That honesty you're encouraging in your child will pay dividends when she stares at you with interest one morning and finally declares, 'I don't like your face.'*

There will also come a time you would pay cash money to not hear the word 'Mummy' for a solid ten minutes.

The pay-off for the incessant chatter is that among the 80,000 words being thrown at you every day, will be some nuggets of such pure gold that you will throw your back out laughing. And I don't care who you are, but the first time your three year old turns to another child and says, 'I'm going to kick your LEGO, mother-f#@&er',* it's really hard not to laugh.

Your job is to get a notebook and write it all down because you'll forget what they said ten minutes after they said it and there's nothing quite like looking back at some of the brilliance your child has shared.

And at least they're not having a tantrum.

*All things real children have said.

# 92

# Words that hurt

'I do it myself' and 'Why?'

Naturally, it's hugely important to raise a confident and independent child with a healthy curiosity and love of learning. It's just a shame it's so bloody annoying.

'I do it myself' would be fine if toddlers could actually do what they say they're going to do in a competent and timely manner.

But they cannot. And you simply cannot tell them otherwise.

'I do it myself' is ALWAYS pulled out when you're in a hurry. ALWAYS. Grown women are brought to tears as they watch their two year old try to do up their own seatbelt, which everyone knows they absolutely *will not* achieve but if you lay a hand on that belt, the screaming that follows will cause permanent damage to your already fragile eardrums.

There is no compromise with a toddler. It's their way or the highway. All you can do is sit by and try to convince them that *you* should do it. It could go a few ways:

1.  She will win and will take 42 minutes to put her own shoes on.
2.  She will relent and ask you to help—after 42 minutes of trying.
3.  You will lose your patience, pick up your child and spike her into the car without her shoes on while the whole neighbour- hood peers through their curtains at that woman traumatising her child AGAIN.

None of these will make you feel like a winner. 'I do it myself' is a lose–lose situation for you until she actually can do it herself—and at that point in time she will lose any interest in doing anything at all for herself ever again.

And then there's 'Why?'

It's a rite of passage for all small children to learn that if they keep saying 'Why?' over and over again until forever, you have to keep answering them. Even if you're hissing, 'I DON'T FECKING KNOOOOW' it doesn't matter, because 'Why?' is like the song that never ends. *You don't fecking knoooow, Mummy? WHY?*

The extra fun part is when they ask questions that don't even have an answer.

'What is that, Mummy?'

'Well, darling, that's a tree.'

'Why?'

'What do you mean *why*? Why is it a tree? It just *is*.'

'Why?'

'Because some things just *are*, okay?'

'Why?'

'Because that's how the world works.'

'Why?'

'I haven't figured that out just yet, sweetheart.'

'Why?'

'Because I'm clearly an idiot.'

'Why?'

'Because I keep answering you!'

'Why?'

'I DON'T KNOW.'

'Why?'

'Please stop asking me why.'

'Okay. Can I have a Milo please?'

'Yes, darling, you can.'

'Why?'

And then you throw an adult tantrum.

# 93

# You're my bess fwend

A toddler throws the 'best friend' title around like confetti.

The first time you hear it, you'll swoon with blessed delight. It's finally happening, your child has noticed how cool you are and has handpicked YOU to be her right-hand woman. You deserve it. You grew that child, you should get a best friend out of the deal. Oh wow, all the fun things you'll be able to do together, babycinos at the cafe, gossip sessions in the park . . .

Until that title is ripped from you like an Olympian on drug charges.

Suddenly, the postman is also her best friend. Tony from next door's dog is her best friend. That eyeless doll with gum in its hair is her best friend. With a sinking heart you realise the title might not mean as much as you thought. I won't lie. It stings.

Although not as much as when the title is taken away because of some arbitrary grievance like saying no to the third cookie. 'You not my bess fwend.'

It's okay, little one, I'm sure the knife in my heart won't leave a scar worse than the one from when they CUT YOU OUT OF MY BODY IN WHICH I GAVE YOU LIFE. No big deal.

True story: *Having a quiet cuddle with my son*

Son: Mummy, I really love you.

Me: *heart goes boom* Oh darling, I really love you too!

Son: You're not my best friend though.

Me: . . .

Son: Daddy is my best friend.

Me: . . . but . . .

Son: I only *love* you.

Me: What about . . .

Son: JUST DADDY.

# 94

# Controlling toddlers

Hahahahahahahaaaa, please tell me you jumped straight to this chapter in the hopes I'd give you some tips on how to control your toddler.

No.

Toddlers are the only humans on the planet who won't be controlled.

Babies? Yeah, babies are pretty dumb, to be honest. Firstly, they can't move very well so you can sit them in a corner, give them a block and you're in control.

Older kids? Harder, for sure, but you can use logic and reason and if that doesn't work you can use bribes and threats. But most importantly, they can talk properly and you can discuss things with them.

Toddlers? No.

They can move, which is significant, so physically controlling them is out—and as we've established, they have zero sense of self-preservation so this can be a crippling flaw in the system.

They're also smart enough to have opinions about life and how they want to live it but they're utterly insane so their opinions are bull and usually dangerous.

Parents of toddlers are often judged (usually by people who don't have children) for what looks like them *letting* their toddler behave like an outlaw. But 'controlling' a toddler is not quite as straightforward as those people might think.

Parents might be able to contain, distract or, if they have advanced skills, manipulate their toddler's behaviour, but control? No. They will not be controlled.

The reason is: toddlers want to fight. From the minute they open their eyes to the minute they close them—and they'll fight about closing them—they want to fight you.

They're on the defence all day long because their lives are filled with NO. And, to be fair, it's a pretty rotten life to live when every desire you have is thwarted (with reason, sure, but still, it can't be fun). So they fight absolutely every decision you make, because, well, it wasn't *their* decision.

So parents of toddlers have two choices. They can argue with their toddlers all day long and live in a house of misery—or they can pick their battles.

Because when all you do is say 'no' to a toddler, they stop hearing it, because that's just that thing you say. But when you save it for when it *really* matters, you've got a better chance of them paying attention.

When you see a two year old in line at the post office, wearing a helmet and a swimming costume? That mother has wisely picked her battles today. Sure mate, great outfit choice, not worth the fight at all.

What people who have no experience with toddlers don't understand is that dealing with a toddler requires patience, creativity, and an insider's knowledge on how much worse the behaviour can get.

So, when they see a three year old at a restaurant, standing on his chair and dumping fistfuls of rice on the table, they might think, 'Tut, what an arsehole, we would NEVER let our child behave like that. Why won't she tell him to sit down?'. But what they don't know—what they can't *understand*—is that mother is doing an amazing job of Containing The Situation because she knows that what her child really wants to do is get down off that chair, run a few laps of the restaurant, scream a little bit and then set fire to something.

So what those childfree people *should* be thinking is THANK YOU. THANK YOU for letting us all eat in peace. THANK YOU for distracting your child with a smaller, less destructive crime. THANK YOU for knowing that forcing a toddler to sit and be still for longer than ten minutes is torture and will likely end in an almighty tantrum.

So, thanks for the judgement and opinions, but toddlers are usually not being naughty, they're just being CHILDREN. We need to stop expecting kids to act like adults. They're not adults, they're kids. And sure, kids can be arseholes—toddlers are the biggest arseholes of them all—but we shouldn't have to keep them locked up at home like criminals. They need to learn how to behave in public and that means being out in public, right next to you and your unreasonable expectations.

# 95

# Sugar and spice

People also have some pretty damaging opinions on how you should raise your children according to their gender.

Even in this day and age, people still think little girls should be cute and sweet. Quiet and polite. They should sit and play with dolls, with their hair neatly tied up and their faces clean.

It was shockingly early in my daughter's life that people started making comments about how she should behave or look because she's a girl.

Taking her out in a blue top caused confusion and disappointment, because BOY COLOUR. Not dressing her in 'girly' clothes seemed to genuinely upset people. The expectation that she should look a certain way, even as a baby, was strong. Before she'd even learnt who she was, she was being told that her appearance was a vital part of her.

I also started to notice how impractical girls' clothes are. Their shorts are so much shorter than boys' shorts. Their tops are so much skimpier. And this starts in babyhood. Why does a twelve month old need denim cut-offs that are so short her nappy hangs out the bottom? Is there a design executive looking at two identical pairs of size 1 shorts and making the decision to 'girlify' the girls' shorts by making them 3 centimetres shorter than the boys'?

Why? Because baby girls need to show more thigh? Why is that cuter? Why do they even need to look cute? Can't they just wear clothes that let them play and explore without worrying about being attractive enough to ADULTS?

Some people tell little girls to be 'ladylike'. They say it's not 'pretty' to be dirty or play with cars. They push and pull these perfect little creatures to behave in the way adults want them to behave.

Hearing other mothers tell their daughters to be quiet, to keep clean and to not ruin their hair makes me so sad to think of all the girls learning that being loud, happy, adventurous, outspoken and funny is bad. Society is so keen to shove little girls into boxes that we extinguish the spark in them before it's even taken hold.

I always thought I was a strong woman and an ardent feminist. Then I had a daughter and the flame in my belly for women's rights became a raging wildfire. I'm so tired of the expectations placed on girls and women to behave a certain way.

*Darling girl,*

*I'll never say you're perfect. No one ever is.*

*There is no 'standard' you'll ever need to meet to be worthy in my eyes.*

*I don't want perfection. I want YOU.*

*I love you exactly as you are right now. I love who you've been and I already love who you'll become.*

*You'll never need to change anything about yourself to make me love you more.*

*But if you changed, I would love you still.*

*And if you broke, I would love all the tiny pieces of you until you stitched yourself back together again. And then I'd love your patchwork soul.*

*If the whole world turned against you, I would be right here, loving you exactly as you are.*

*I love your sass, I love your fire. I love your peace, your compassion and your kindness. I love your funny, your crazy and your weird. I love your face and your heart and your soul.*

*Baby girl, please hear this: you don't have to be 'careful'. You don't have to be quiet or calm; you don't have to be neat and tidy. You don't need to be 'pretty' or 'sweet'. You don't need to be anybody's dress-up doll or a goddamn 'good girl'.*

*You are way too magical to fit inside a box.*

*Be WILD, my daughter. Be LOUD. Explore, have adventures, climb trees and mountains. Take risks. TAKE UP ROOM.*

*Say no when you want, say yes when you want. Try new things. Wear what you like, say what you think. Be proud of yourself for winning. Laugh at and learn from your failures.*

*SHINE. Never apologise for it. Never make yourself small for someone else.*

*Hold on to your wild, my darling. Keep it and use it and never let it go. The world will tell you to leave it behind as you grow but your wild is your strength and you're going to need it.*

*I'm telling you this now because sometimes I might forget how to be the mother you need . . . because I'm not perfect either.*

*But I've never wanted to try so hard at anything in my life.*

*You, baby girl, were born with the fire, and I will be your oxygen.*

*I love you.*

*Love Mummy xxx*

# 96

# Slugs and snails

Society feels even more uncomfortable about little boys 'not acting like boys'.

The faces if you dare dress your boy in pink ... straight-up confusion. Their brains will not compute and they'll scramble to come up with some excuse for why you were forced to put this wee little man in a 'girl's colour'. Perhaps you are poor and cannot afford clothes and these were things given to you by a charity? Perhaps you aren't quite stable and you need a lie-down because, sweet mumma, you've dressed your BOY in PINK. Did you notice that?

Little boys are sensitive souls. They feel things just like we do. But society wants them to *not* feel things. Boys shouldn't cry. They shouldn't whinge or complain. They shouldn't feel pain when they fall over. They shouldn't need comfort and cuddles. They're just tiny little boys—*babies*—who need their mum's cuddles just as much as little girls do, who feel that graze on their knee like anyone else would, who get scared of loud noises and new places just like any child would. Yet adults get annoyed if they cry.

Little boys who are taught not to bother anyone with their feelings are boys who grow up unable to ask for help when those feelings start to drag them under.

Or they stuff their feelings down deep until they don't even know what to do with them except *hit*.

Little boys who don't know how to manage their emotions become big boys who throw coward punches in pubs. Because those big boys are feeling big emotions but they've never understood or been able to deal with those feelings—so they lash out. They're just angry little boys who never grew up.

But we tell boys that showing emotion is girly. 'Stop acting like a girl', people will say.

When I hear this said to a little boy, it makes me want to roundhouse-kick the dickhead who said it, straight in the windpipe. Don't even get me started on what I want to do when I hear them say this in front of THEIR DAUGHTER.

You know what this says to a little boy?

It says to him that girls are weak and silly. Girls are whiny and annoying. Girls are 'less than' boys. Acting like a girl is the worst thing you can do.

So that little boy grows up believing that being a boy is infinitely better than being a girl, with the added bonus of learning that to 'be a man' he should never show emotion.

Has anyone ever said to a girl, 'Stop acting like a boy'?

What the hell is wrong with acting like a girl?

I'm a girl and I'M SENSATIONAL.

Boys need to be allowed to feel things, they need to be allowed to play with dolls and 'girl' toys because it's how they express their caring side.

Little boys love playing with dolls because they want to be like mum. They watch mum wrap up babies, and cuddle and love them, and they want to be like her. Their little hearts are caring and nurturing and they want to show that through imaginative play.

'Caring' isn't a 'woman's job' unless we tell little boys it is. Being tender, sweet and considerate isn't shameful or weird and boys don't need to smash things up to be a 'boy'.

What harm is being done to a little boy who is learning how to *care*? What are we so afraid will happen? That boys will become soft? That they'll learn to show empathy and tenderness to people? How terrifying.

*Darling boy,*

*I want you to be happy, most of all. But I'll never turn away from you if you're sad. I'll never tell you not to feel angry. I'll never be disappointed in you if you're scared.*

*I can't carry your emotions for you but you won't ever have to travel through them alone. I'll forever walk beside you, sharing your anger, your joy and your fear. It's my job. I love you.*

*I love how big you feel things. And I will protect your right to show it, for as long as you'll let me.*

*Your sensitive soul, your gentleness, your compassion and your kindness—these are the very best parts of you. Don't ever hide them away. Being a 'man' doesn't mean hiding your heart, it means having no fear in sharing it.*

*And your heart is your strength.*

*It makes you a wonderful friend because you have empathy for other people.*

*It makes you smart and observant because you see all the possibilities laid out in front of you before you take your first steps.*

*You have no instinct to hurt people and this will keep you safe in life. People who swing before they think never win. Walking away is the smartest thing you'll ever do and I'm so glad that's how you're built.*

*My sweet boy, you don't have to be tough. You don't have to be rough. You don't need to be loud or bold if you don't want to be. You don't need to 'man up' or take it on the chin. It's not your job to hide your feelings to make other people feel comfortable.*

*Be kind, be caring, be gentle and sweet. Use your words. Tell me everything.*

*That's how you'll change the world, my darling. You're a thinker and a planner and you like to know all the information before you do anything.*

*I want you to know how proud I am of you and how hard I see you work. You are everything I want—and more. And you'll never need to change to make me happy.*

*You were born with a heart, my boy, and I never want you to hide it.*

*I love you.*

*Love Mummy xxx*

# 97

# Seeing the world for the first time

The greatest joy of living with toddlers is seeing the world through their eyes for the first time. You relearn all the things about life you'd stopped even caring about.

Your hard exterior, built up over the years of being an adult—of having your heart broken, being disappointed over and over again, seeing all the pain in the world—starts to break away and you wonder when you became so cynical. Now, with this two year old by your side, you're seeing the wonder in things you've never noticed before.

The first taste of ice cream. The first concert. The first time they truly understand that some people speak a different language to them. You can see, as clear as if they were slotting the final piece of the puzzle in place, the realisation dawn on their face and you wonder about the process it took to get them there. Then you try to imagine what it must be like to learn something, anything for the very first time.

You see the delight over a rainbow. They shriek and jump up and down and wave their arms and you smile at how the smallest things can make them so happy, but then they look to you to see if you're seeing what they're seeing and suddenly you realise that rainbow isn't a small thing at all—it's actually the loveliest thing ever. How could you have forgotten that?

One day your child will tell you how planes in the sky are going very fast but they look slow from down on the ground because we are so far away and you'll think, 'Who taught you that?' And the answer is: no one. He figured it out by himself, because kids are so much smarter than you give them credit for.

It's rewards like this that make all the hard parts worth it. You will want to grab their dimpled little hand and set off on an endless adventure because life is simply sweeter when you're experiencing it with a curious toddler.

# 98

# They just wanna be excited

Toddlers get themselves super hyped-up about the smallest things. They're dying to be excited about life. They spend all day looking around and waiting to be amazed and fascinated. You should exploit this as much as you can.

Sure, this sounds a bit sketchy but if you're going to bring joy, you might as well bring joy to your child AND yourself.

It's all in the way you say it.

You could say, 'Time to pack up!' and you would be speaking to the ether.

Or you could say, 'Hey, who wants to help Mummy PACK . . . THINGS . . . UUUUUPPPPP?' and your child will come running like you're Larry Emdur on *The Price is Right*.

The thing is, when your toddler gets all wild-eyed-thrilled about something truly mundane, you can't help but get excited about it too. Toddlers are infectious. And yeah, I mean that in all senses of the word, too. They're also walking Petri dishes of bacteria and you'll catch everything from them. But mostly you'll catch feels. Good ones. And bad ones. But let's focus on the good ones right now.

# 99

# And so you should travel with them

Travelling with toddlers is not usually recommended. They're as crazy and loud as they always are and putting them in a flying metal tube is torturous for you and everyone else travelling alongside you. When you reach your destination, there is no downtime. It's the exact same stuff you do at home, but in a different location, without all the comforts of your stuff, and with the added bonus of sitting in a dark room every night from 7 p.m. instead of hitting the town.

However, if you can accept that you won't be relaxing like you did on the holidays of your youth, you will find that a toddler can make your holiday magical.

We took our son to Fiji when he was two. Yes, he needed naps in the middle of the day, yes he was out of sorts at bedtime, yes he made meals hectic, BUT . . .

Every night they had a fire-lighting ceremony at the resort. Men dressed in traditional costumes would walk around lighting torches to the beat of tribal drums. It was charming and all the guests enjoyed it, but NO ONE loved it as much as my son. He squealed and jumped up and down like he was seeing flying dinosaurs or riding a fire engine down a rainbow. His pure and unadulterated joy at seeing the fire ceremony every night was the best part of our trip by far.

I looked at all the faces of older kids and adults who sat quietly and watched the show and felt so sad that we'd all lost the spark of wonder we'd had as toddlers. We don't whoop and jump with happiness because we've become self-conscious and indifferent to life's marvels.

We live a life of restraint and responsibility, but then we have a child and for this very brief time we allow ourselves to share their delight. We let ourselves whoop and jump, and fling our hands to the sky, because how can we not? When a two year old is vibrating with joy, how can we ignore it? We simply have to join their joy train and ride it with them.

Sure, holidays won't involve lazing on the beach all day and drinking all night, but you will find the twinkle in things you wouldn't have noticed without your little spark beside you. It's even worth a plane trip. Trust me.

# 100

# These are things you say now

If you have spent a lot of time reading parenting blogs, you might think the most common phrases to come out of a parent's mouth are things like:

- 'I love you to the moon and back.'
- 'You are my world.'
- 'I am so blessed.'
- 'Let's make dolls' dresses together out of this botanically hand-dyed linen I made.'

No. Mothers of toddlers aren't saying these things in real life. Mothers of toddlers would love to say these things but mothers of toddlers are far too busy repeating the same things over and over and over and over again, like:

- 'No.'
- 'I said NO.'
- 'Get down from there.'
- 'SIT. Bottom on the seat, thank you.'
- 'Why is this wet? What is this?'
- 'PLEASE don't tip it all out on the floor. PLEEEEASE.'
- 'What's in your mouth? Open your mouth.'
- 'Where did you get that?'
- 'Why are you naked?'
- 'Why are you licking that?'
- 'You love pasta. Please eat it.'
- 'Where are you?'
- 'I'm just doing a poo, okay?'
- 'Can you please wait one minute?'
- 'Half a minute?'
- 'I'm doing it RIGHT NOW. Can you not see me doing it, right in front of you? Please stop asking me to do it.'
- 'Can you please get your penis out of that?'
- 'We don't stick pencils in cats' bottoms.'

# 101

# Kids' books and TV

You'll also now know more than is fit for an adult to know about children's television and books. The most passionate discussions you'll have with other parents is which TV character you loathe the most and which fairy tale is the most disturbing.

For the record, mine are: Bing, the pathologically whiny bunny, and the original Rapunzel where she's dumped in a desert for being a ho, and her boyfriend is blinded by thorns and left to wander the backwoods for years as a beggar. Sweet dreams, kids!

Despite all the warnings about screen time turning your precious child into Sloth from The Goonies, you will form an amiable, co-parenting relationship with the television and its unmatched ability to keep your juvenile delinquent still and silent for whole MINUTES at a time.

It does, however, mean you will be exposed to some of the most painful 'entertainment' ever created.

Like *Yo Gabba Gabba*, which is, as far as I can tell, the adventures of a grown man who carries around a suitcase filled with animated sex toys.

Or *In The Night Garden*, which is, for all intents and purposes, a glance inside the acid-fuelled nightmares of a bunch of psychology students who are clearly using our children as test subjects for a study into subliminal warfare.

There's *Bananas in Pyjamas*, the very sad tale of a couple of mentally challenged anthropomorphised fruit people, who routinely mangle the most simple of tasks only to be taken advantage of by their 'friend'—the most malicious, conniving and self-centred Rat you'll ever meet.

And of course, there's *Bing*, the pathetically inept bunny who will teach your children the value of whining incessantly until a disturbingly small ragdoll guardian creature steps up to explain how to not be a frigging moron and cleans up all his messes.

Don't even get me started on *Hoopla Doopla* and the deeply unnerving compound in which these mute clowns live and work, with seemingly no contact with the outside world and no way in which to communicate other than mediocre stunts and slapstick banality.

You might think reading is a safer pastime but on closer inspection, you'll find books aren't always the answer either.

We've got *Where is The Green Sheep?*, where kids will learn to ignore the desperate cries of the community who are clearly concerned for their whereabouts.

There's *The Very Hungry Caterpillar*, which will make your children believe that eating until you slip into a coma will give you wings.

What about the Aussie classic *The Very Cranky Bear*, in which a turgid bully threatens and demeans a bunch of friends until a poor little sheep disfigures herself by shaving off half her wool so he'll leave them alone for a few minutes? Excellent life lesson for kids there.

But worst of all is the Dr Seuss classic *The Cat in the Hat*. A Cat man preys on two children whose mother has left them alone and unsupervised and forces them to engage in a variety of increasingly unpleasant activities. They clearly don't want to get involved but they are at the mercy of this stranger, who is probably on some sort of watchlist somewhere.

It should be noted that Dr Seuss was not actually a doctor. It was a self-appointed title. Which makes sense.

Once you enter this world, you will find yourself enraged, appalled, alarmingly invested and worryingly knowledgeable about characters you'll know on a first-name basis: Peppa, Thomas, Bluey, Duggee, Ben and Holly.

But not enough to turn the TV off. That would just be madness.

# 102

# From baby to actual person

Toddlerhood is the time you'll see your child's true personality come to the fore, offering a glimpse of who they might be when they grow up.

You'll see how all those times you made them say 'please' has paid off. You'll see them put their bowl in the sink and do a happy dance because all that encouragement is working. You'll see them show kindness to another child and be so damn proud because YOU taught them that.

You'll see all the characteristics you hoped you'd pass on to your child: confidence, determination, a strong sense of right and wrong, a take-no-prisoners zest for life and a refusal to care what anyone else thinks.

You're so proud. You admire all of these qualities.

You are so dumb for realising how hard this would make your life.

Yes, you want your child to be confident. But could they be confident at a lower volume, and maybe with fewer words and a tiny bit of respect for the fact you might know *some* things?

Yes, you want your child to be determined. Unless *you're* trying to get them to do *anything*. Anything at all.

Yes, you want your child to have a strong sense of right and wrong ... when they figure out what is actually right and wrong and not when they are arguing with the fervour of a meth-head that having a bath is the wrongest of the wrongs.

Of course you want your child to take no prisoners. One day. Not today, when you're the one in the firing line.

You absolutely want your child to be a free spirit who doesn't care what anyone else thinks. In the future, though, because right now she really needs to care that you think it's time for bed.

And while you've been actively trying to influence your child to copy all your good traits, you'll soon realise that they've been watching EVERYTHING. All the time. Including all the things you never wanted them to learn.

Like when your child rolls his eyes and talks about those 'wankers' across the road who don't know how to park their car.

Or when your three year old struggles to open a box, sighs and mutters to himself, 'For f#@&'s sake, why aren't I getting this?'

Or when your mini-me disciplines you with your own words: 'We don't yell in this house, Mummy!' Rightio, goody-two-shoes.

Or when your former baby argues with you and her point is completely valid and the horror hits you: this is a person with opinions and ideas and a right to express them and holy mother of god, why are you questioning my decisions? Surely I am owed more time as the omnipotent one in this house? RESPECT MY AUTHORITY, SMALL CHILD!

But you'll also see how much good your influence can do.

My daughter and I were walking home, my son and husband not far behind us. My little girl told me, with a touch of defeat in her voice, that the boys would beat us home. I looked at my tiny three year old and said with a grin, 'NO WAY. We are GIRLS. We are SUPERGIRLS! We are FAST AND STRONG!' and I held up my non-existent bicep to show her.

Right before my eyes I saw my daughter change: from a girl who'd somehow already got it in her head that boys were faster than girls to a SUPERGIRL. Her gloomy little eyes smiled with hope: *Really? Are we supergirls?* Her mouth twitched: *I can't believe it—that's so cool!*

'Supergirls?' she asked, excitement building.

'SUPERGIRLS!' I yelled. 'FAST AND STRONG.'

'FAST AND STRONG!' she yelled back.

And of course we beat those boys home.

The next day I'd forgotten all about it when she walked up to me and whispered, 'You say it, Mummy.'

'Say what, darling?'

'*Supergirls,*' she said, with a twinkle in her eyes.

I leapt up, non-biceps blazing, leading the chorus 'WE ARE SUPERGIRLS, FAST AND STRONG!'

She'd remembered. It had made an impact. With a few little words, her thinking had started to change. That's all it takes some-times—a few little words and they're bumped onto a different path that stretches out for years to come.

It's empowering, it's exciting, and it's actually the most terrify-ing part of parenting: all the tiny ways we can change them. And all the tiny ways we can stuff them up.

# 103

# Actual insanity

Of course, this makes it all the more difficult when your child comes at you with something so irrational and illogical that it makes your brain hurt.

Isn't this the child who just showed a startling level of maturity and consideration?

So WHY is she now on the floor, kicking the wall and pulling her own hair because I asked her to not wee on the couch?

WHAT IS GOING ON?

You're making lunch and she says she wants a Vegemite sandwich and you make her a Vegemite sandwich and now she's convulsing in her chair.

Is it the bread? The colour of the plate? Did she want the crusts off?

HELP ME UNDERSTAND.

You suggest some time to play outside and she kicks her plate straight to the floor and a vein in her forehead pops out from the force of her scream and it takes a good ten minutes for it to settle down.

HOW DO I MAKE THIS STOP?

Yeah, you can't.

Life is a constant dance across eggshells with toddlers as you do your best to keep them calm and happy—but also not let them become unmitigated a-holes. It takes skill. It takes intelligence, patience, negotiation finesse, powers of persuasion, mind games and straight-up bribery.

It's the most exhausting part of parenthood yet.

It's hard not to feel sorry for them sometimes, especially when getting what they want somehow enrages them. Like: okay, you want a bowl of grapes—here you go, darling. Oh, wait, you're now livid because I've given you the bowl of grapes that you asked for? No big deal, that's my fault—sincere apologies. I'll take my leave.

You won't be able to help yourself, though: you'll try to argue with them using logical reasoning. Even though you know it's point-less, it will achieve nothing and it will probably make things worse.

It's like picking a fight with a brick wall. Why would you do that? It's a wall. You're going to hurt yourself. But you do it anyway because it seems that you too have lost your freaking mind.

We know that toddlers are incapable of understanding logic. You will point at the road and say, 'We do not walk on the road because it's dangerous and you could be hurt' and they'll walk straight at the road. Why? Because their brains told them to.

A toddler's brain hears things, throws those things through a shredder and then pieces them back together like an abstract expressionist.

You say, 'Please don't lick the floor' and they hear 'Please lick the floor and also my leg'.

You say, 'Please put on your pants' and they hear 'Please run, run, run as fast as you can'.

You say, 'It's time for bed' and they hear 'It's time for bed, where your life will most likely end in a slow and torturous death while I stand by and watch, probably eating the popcorn I said you couldn't have earlier today'.

Do not even hint at something that might happen in the distant future because your child will hear it as a BLOOD OATH. The other day I told my son that if he carried on when I took the iPad away, I wouldn't let him watch it tomorrow. Somehow, he heard, 'I promise, on my life, and without restriction, that you can watch the iPad tomorrow' and no amount of dissecting the actual words I used will convince him otherwise.

Sometimes it's incredibly hard not to laugh at the intensity and insanity of their tantrums, but even if it feels like they're crying for no goddamn reason, it feels life-or-death important to them. Give them a little hug while they lose their mind over the fact that the time is now 4 o'clock and they wanted it to be 3 o'clock. And try to keep your giggling behind their back.

# 104

# The rage of motherhood

Pressing our buttons. It's their special skill.

They know exactly what's going to send you right over the edge and they'll do it repeatedly until you, a fully grown adult, dissolve into rage. Against a toddler. Who even *are* you now?

We should be able to rise above it. This is our *child*. This is the baby we cradled at night, whispering lullabies and promising we'd never stop loving them. This is the child we looked at and thought, 'How could I ever be mad at you?'

But now you have moments where you look at your child and mutter, 'No, really, what the hell is *wrong* with you?'

Having the patience to deal with a toddler day in and day out is not a skill any humans possess, so don't feel guilty if you lose your biscuits occasionally. It happens to the best of us: that uncontrollable, irrational rage that explodes from nowhere. You'll feel guilty immediately because it really didn't warrant that sort of response, but they just PRESSED. YOUR. BUTTONS.

And it could be for a reason that is so tiny, so silly, so benign that you're almost embarrassed to admit it.

It's okay—you're not alone. We've all got our 'thing'.

I asked some real mums to tell me their trigger points and this is what they said:

- when he touches me around the neck area
- when she breathes on my neck
- when they can see I'm on the phone but start demanding all the things
- when he dawdles—like practically moves in slow motion—and nothing I say has any effect
- when they touch me with their toenails
- when he asks me a question but doesn't listen to the answer
- when they ask me repeatedly to do something when I've asked them to wait. I've heard you, I'll do it, just wait!
- when she stands right in front of the door as I'm trying to open it
- when he starts a sentence with, 'Mum, can I tell you something?' JUST TELL ME!
- when she drinks the bathwater after I've said for the fiftieth time not to drink the bathwater
- when she sits on the toilet and hugs the whole goddamn seat then slouches down and holds her face with her toilet hands
- when he leans on my head when I'm putting on his shoes. OMFG! Just stand up!
- when he sticks his elbow in my boob, stomach or thigh to push himself up
- when they say 'Mum' repeatedly even though I've already answered
- when they step on my toes or the top of my feet
- when they make ALL. THE. NOISE just for shiz and giggles

- when they tap, tug, pull on my clothes—basically any sort of repetitive touching
- when she ignores me or pretends not to hear me
- when she fake-cries or puts on a baby voice.

See? We've all got those little things that send us over the edge. They're the love of your life but no one will make you fume like your own child.

# 105

# I yelled today

*I yelled at you today.*

*You were doing something I'd asked you not to do about four or five times already.*

*The final time you looked me dead in the eye as I spoke and you did it again.*

*Maaate, the snap was like Britney feat. umbrella c. 2007.*

*I felt bad as soon as the words were out, but I didn't stop. My mouth has always had one speed and my brain another. It takes a while for my brain to catch my mouth and hiss-whisper, 'Shut up, Lauren, it's done.' Ask any of my bosses, ever.*

*The first yell was because you clearly function at a different frequency to other humans. The only time you acknowledge that I've spoken is if I break 90 decibels or more.*

*The second yell was because you didn't transform into an obedient child within 0.3 seconds of the first yell. Yes, I know that's completely unfair but that's how my rage works; I require immediate results. It's quite incompatible with motherhood.*

*The third and maybe fourth yell weren't about you at all, to be honest—they were about me. A lot of the time it's about me.*

*I'm yelling because I'm frustrated—which frustrates me because I'm a goddamn adult and you're three so clearly I hold the wit and reason in this relationship . . . or do I?*

*I'm yelling because I feel like I should be able to get you to listen and I can't remember a single word of the 768 articles I've saved about getting children to listen without yelling.*

*I'm yelling about my failure to not be the yelly mum. I want to be the Zen mum who connects with her child on a spiritual level, so they don't even need to use words to understand what is and isn't okay. Of course, that'd require you to stop yelling for a minute too.*

*I'm yelling because I'm SO TIRED and, honestly, that's mostly your fault. You're like the mail sorting centre. You. Never. Stop. This is why they call it 'going postal'.*

*But that's no excuse, so I'm sorry. I want you to be a good kid, and it annoys me that I don't know how to do it better and every time I explode, I'm reminded that I'm not as talented as I think.*

*So please remember that I love you and when I yell, it's mostly about 'me and my shortcomings'.*

*And sometimes, it's just a little bit about 'you being a jerk'.*

*Love Mummy xxx*

# 106

# Cherish every moment

You know what's super unenjoyable? Being told to enjoy some-thing. It's a bit like being told to calm down. If I'm having a brain-popping rage attack and you tell me to calm down, you might as well add '. . . and then set fire to my car' because the end result will be much the same.

So when some sweet, well-meaning older lady observes my children as they prepare to engage in the seventy-sixth Hunger Games on the floor of the fruit and veg section and titters, 'Cherish every moment!', it's touch-and-go: will I muster a non-committal, doesn't-reach-the-eyes smile, or will I just pick her up and throw her into the arena with the kids?

'It goes so fast,' she breathes, misty eyed, tilted head, hands to heart. It's always the same. I know those people mean well. They've been there. They know how fast it all goes and how much I'll miss it when my kids grow up. I know it too. I know I'll sob when I think about how precious these days were. But when you're past the stage of poo and tears and screaming, you tend to forget that some of these years are actual douchery.

These people think they're letting mums know how lucky they are, and some women will take it as a sweet moment of connection between generations. But if a mum is struggling, she might take it in a very different way.

## It's too much pressure

As if mums need one more thing to fail at, now we're adding 'showing gratitude' to the list? All day long, I'm looking at my kids, thinking, am I cherishing this enough? Why can't I be more #inthe-moment? What's wrong with me?

Mothers are under pressure to provide educational, sensory-rich, nutrient-dense, character-building experiences for our children—and we have to enjoy it all too? There's no question we enjoy our kids; we love them. But there are moments—lots and lots of moments—where it feels like tedious, repetitive grunt work. It's not as complicated as raising older kids, but it's exhausting.

## It's stupidly unrealistic

I've literally been told to 'even enjoy their tantrums'. What psycho-path enjoys tantrums? Is there something I'm missing? A child in distress is something to be *enjoyed*?

Some aspects of raising small children are decidedly unen-joyable: sleepless nights, sick babies, dinnertime, FAECES. Yes, in hindsight you can look back and think how beautiful it was when your child needed you, but when you're in the moment, and your child is screeching at a pitch that would deafen dachshunds, it's completely acceptable to wish you were sipping mai tais on Maui.

# It's bad advice

Human emotions don't work without the ups and the downs; there's no good without the bad. If you spent all day cherishing every moment, nothing would be special. And I'd question your sanity. Like, how fat's your baby scrapbook FFS? Because we all know you've got one #makingmemories.

If you haven't had a bastard of a day, it doesn't feel quite as special when your toddler wraps her chubby arms around your neck and says, 'You pitty, Mummy'. That's the meaning of motherhood right there. That's what makes us do it and keep doing it—the highs that come after the lows.

# It's unfairly critical

Thanks for the guilt trip, kindly onlooker! The underlying message is: you obviously don't love your children enough. Every mother knows you can be consumed with love for your children and yet, well . . . not like them very much sometimes.

When you're telling mums to cherish every moment, what you're really saying is 'Don't complain'. Which means we're not allowed to admit when we're struggling or need help. It's completely normal to feel overwhelmed, but when we're told we should be cherishing every second, it feels like there's something wrong with us and that's where the spiral of self-doubt begins.

Trust me when I say I'm cherishing the moments that deserve to be cherished. The sweet cuddles, the funny things they say, the flowers picked just for Mummy. I squeeze my eyes shut and compel my brain to remember them like this. I know how fast they're growing; it's agony at times, knowing how much I'll miss it all.

But I'm not going to cherish every moment and you don't have to either. Raising kids is hard and there's nothing weird or wrong with you if you don't like every minute.

# 107

# That don't impress me much

Likewise, you don't have to think your child is special all of the time. Most of the time, toddlers are not that impressive. I mean, they're amazing—to you—but they don't have a lot of *true* talent just yet.

Nevertheless, they'll want you to watch and clap and cheer for EVERYTHING THEY DO.

They'll call out your name over and over and over again:

*Mummy.*

*Mummy.*

*Mum.*

*Mum.*

*Mum!*

*Muuuummmmyyyy!*

*WATCH MEEEEEE!*

The chances they'll actually be doing something impressive when you turn around are slim.

It's okay to not think they're amazing all the time. There are mothers and fathers all around the world, right now, looking at their beloved three year olds, thinking, 'You know what? He's a bit of a penis.'

See? You're not alone.

Sometimes the simplest things they do *are* incredible. Like watching a toddler learn to jump when they're not actually leaving the ground, and you wish you could remember ever feeling that chuffed with your own efforts.

But, more often than not, what they're doing is not worth the admission price.

So when your child yells for the fifteenth time to watch them eat a bowl of cereal, it's okay to be indifferent.

It's totally normal to watch your kid zoom a car along the bench and think, 'No, child, that was not as advertised. I love you, but try harder next time.'

You're not a monster if you don't squeal with delight every time your daughter makes you watch her kick the air.

If you can clap and applaud your child's every fart and burp, I'm happy for you but you're not normal. Perhaps you don't understand what true talent and entertainment value are.

# 108

# The displeased toddler

Besides, it's not like they're always that pleased with you. No one has more contempt than a two year old, which is surprising because, like, how long have you been alive? What life experiences are you basing your judgements on? Stop being such a judgemental flog.

*Dear Mummy,*

*Sometimes you make poor choices but I'm willing to lend you a hand. Here are some areas of improvement for you to consider.*

*If you want me to do whatever you want, just feed me biscuits. It's really that simple.*

*When you sit there on your phone and hand me over to our live-in nanny (aka the TV), you are supposed to feel guilty. Having a cup of tea and putting your feet up makes you look worse. All the other mums are making fruit platters and setting up finger-painting stations, just so you know. Like I'm not saying you should turn the TV off, because you know neither of us wants that; I'm just saying you could act more stressed about it.*

*You should probably sing to me. And dance now and then. Everyone on TV is singing and dancing, and I don't see you do that. I think it would improve our relationship. I like the girl with the bow on her head. Get a bow.*

*If you'd like me to stop climbing things, you should probably remove all the furniture. Alternatively, if you're so concerned about me falling, you should make everything soft and bouncy like a jumping castle. We should probably just move into a jumping castle. Get one with a slide.*

*Stop with the peas.*

*Make toothpaste taste like ice cream, and I might let you brush my teeth. Quick observation: baring all your teeth and growling doesn't make the bathroom feel like a safe space.*

*Loosen your grip on things. People are what's important. You're so attached to your material possessions. I think your life would be better if you just gave stuff to me. Honestly, your phone isn't going to keep you warm at night. But I could keep you warm, Mummy . . . like maybe I should just sleep in your bed? Let's do that tonight and then forever.*

*Love you xxx*

# 109

# Lord of the flies

It's critical to remember that the child you have at five months old is not the same as the child you have at fifteen months old.

The key difference here is MOVEMENT.

A stationary child is perfection. They sit, they smile, they let you clean without interference. Heavenly.

A moving child is a nightmare on legs. They run, they destroy, they undo everything you do the second after you did it.

When you have a five month old who sits and smiles, it's quite easy to keep a nice clean home. It's understandable how you could walk into a friend's house and judge her and her Lord of the Flies children. 'How hard is it, Melissa? You filthy broad.'

Give her a break. Poor old Melissa has *moving* children.

When your child starts to move, you won't stand a chance of keeping things tidy. Even if you removed every item from your home and lived in an empty shell, your child would smuggle in rocks from outside and scatter them around like tiny shards of rebellion digging into the soft underbelly of your poor, tender feet.

We've established that children enjoy the putting of all the things on the floor. Children also spill things. All the things. Even things with lids will somehow find a way to spill. Food, drinks, nappies. All on the floor. They also love to break things and rub filthy hands on things and lick ALL THE THINGS.

It's adorable of you to think you'd be able to keep on top of it. That every time something was put on the floor, you'd be there to grab it and put it back in its rightful place.

Let's imagine that universe.

Your only job is to replace what your child has pulled out. You cannot go to the toilet. You cannot make food. You cannot turn your head. You cannot do a damned thing all day except put away what your child has pulled out.

At some point in the day you leave some of the things for a few minutes so you can get something else done. You'll get back to it later, you tell yourself. But later comes and your child drops his nappy, and a turd rolls onto the kitchen floor. Obviously, that takes priority. So you deal with that while he pulls out some more things.

A little bit later, you try to get back to the tidying, but your child is hungry. And tired. And demands a ball you don't even own, and screams at you for 24 minutes. And the phone rings. And later never comes. And by the time he goes to bed, he's created seventeen times more mess than you started with, and you have a little sob, grab a glass of wine and sit down to watch TV because you've earned it.

And this is why our homes look like a scene from *Lord of the Flies*. Unless we have people coming over, and then we throw everything into a washing basket and chuck it in a garage or cupboard five minutes before they arrive. Tada!

# 110

# Toilet-training delights

Ah toddlerhood, the time has come. Your house is now marinated in a light coating of urine, with the aroma of hidden poo adding that extra zest. Yes. Bare naked poo. Lying on the floor, among your velvet throw cushions and hardcover books.

You are now a person who has staged a very involved Ted Talk in your home, titled, 'How to know when the poo is coming'.

You now know that children can develop a deep, dark phobia of letting their poo drop into the toilet and you spend your days chasing your child around the house, imploring him to let go of the steaming fresh bounty in his pants and trying to understand how any human could want a juicy bog smeared between their cheeks. You've even stooped to showing your child how happy you are to flush your own poo away. 'Look, there's Mummy's poo! Yes, thank you, it is a big one—I worked hard on it. Now let's flush it away! Bye bye poo poo!' Ahh, if your old drinking mates could see you now.

Don't be afraid of toilet training. No, you won't become more patient or understanding. You won't suddenly develop a tolerance for turd. You won't develop any insight into how your toddler's brain actually works. But you *will* gain at least one fantastic story you can share for years to come.

Like this one. It's based on a true story, told to me by a friend. Oh, how I wish it were mine.

———————

We were in the throes of toilet training and my little boy was doing well with the wees and we were putting in a lot of work for the poo on the potty.

I was in the kitchen cooking dinner when my boy walked in, completely naked, brandishing a small square of tissue smeared brown.

It's a funny thing when you're simultaneously over-the-moon-proud because your child not only defecated but tried to wipe his own bum—and also frantically anxious about how accurate his wiping has been.

I ran over to the potty and saw that he had indeed backed out an enormous, adult-sized log into the potty. The poo dance followed, naturally. Because we celebrate poo. Then I jogged off to get some wipes to clean up his hands, bum, legs and, curiously, a little bit on his neck.

By the time he was clean and I'd washed my hands for the fourth time, I turned to get the potty and saw it was empty.

Now I might be a busy, harassed, overworked mother, but even I wouldn't have imagined a huge turd that wasn't really there. I doubted myself for a fraction of a second before I told myself that I'd just spent a good few minutes cleaning the skid marks off my child. There had definitely been a poo.

I turned to my child and asked him where it was.

'Where did your poo go, mate?'

I was once a successful, professional woman. I did presentations on end-of-year financial reports. I supervised a team of twelve. Never did I imagine I would one day utter those words. And yet there I was.

He looked at me and said he didn't know. I asked again, a little more manically this time.

'Darling, please think. Did you put your poo somewhere?'

He shook his head again. With just the two of us in the house, I had to take his word for it. My two year old was my only ally against this mounting emergency. I had to keep him onside.

My eyes swung wildly from wall to wall, searching for any sign of the missing poo.

A missing poo is not something you can write off with a shrug and an 'Oh, well'. A missing poo must be found. Poos don't get better with time.

I HAD to find this poo.

I began ransacking my own house—pulling up rugs, looking behind curtains, trying to piece together a timeline that would help me pinpoint the moment it went missing, trying to work out the logistics of how it possibly got out of the potty, visualising it flinging itself out of the bowl and rolling to freedom.

But if it had rolled anywhere, surely it would leave a trail. The floor didn't show a mark. How would it even start to roll? There HAD to be an accomplice.

I ran through the possible suspects.

It wasn't me. I'm fairly sure.

My gut told me it wasn't my son. He showed no signs of enjoying this dung hunt and he'd been by my side the whole time. I'm his alibi.

There were no other humans in the whole house.

But . . . we weren't alone. There were two dogs.

I turned to look at them. One: lazing on the carpet, ear flicking in the breeze. The other: sitting up. Eyes locked on mine. Shame written all over his face.

I picked him up and the fumes rolled off him in waves, smacking me straight in the nose.

I just made it to the back door before I dry-retched in horror. I dropped the dog outside and slammed the door shut. His guilty little face stared through the glass. He knew what he'd done.

He'd polished the whole thing off. Licked the bowl clean. A steaming meal for one.

———————

So when you're worried you don't have any interesting stories anymore because you're just a mum, remember: there's always toilet training.

# 111

# The favourite parent

Your child will love you more than any other human in the world. Your koala's world will revolve around you, her light, her source of love and care—until she becomes a toddler.

This child who ran to you for every tiny need in her life because you grew her and fed her and kept her alive for so long . . . she has discovered Daddy.

You love your partner, you feel like a team, you want to be his equal in all parts of parenting.

But one day you'll spend nine hours straight running after your child, setting up activities, making all the food, singing songs and reading books and just generally being a boss.

Then he'll waltz in. Do a wiggly arm movement and your child will light up like she's just seen the face of God and she will drop you like the hot garbage you are. Clearly this man is a ball bag. He's a traitor and a scoundrel who will never once try to play it cool to make you look good because he secretly loves being the favourite.

It honestly makes me wonder why mothers have traditionally been the primary caregiver; because it seems that children universally prefer men over women.

It's not that kids don't like women. They think women are perfectly acceptable and might even enjoy spending time with us. But if they had a choice, they'd choose to hang out with blokes. Every time.

Look, I'm not going to theorise about why this is. A more bitter woman might say something like, 'it makes sense because men are basically extra large children so they think like three year olds all day long,' but I'd never suggest that. And I'd never suggest it's because men can give kids their full attention when they're together; whereas women are playing trains while menu-planning, folding laundry, writing to-do lists in their minds, answering work emails behind their kids' backs, etc.

So yeah, I have no idea why kids gravitate towards men. And I'm not bothered by it at all. Just gave them life, you know? No big deal. Just cater to their every need and desire. It's totally fine. Just work myself into the ground every single waking hour trying to make them happy, I'M REALLY OKAY ABOUT THIS.

It's also entirely possible your child will like their grandparents more than you. But this makes total sense because your parents' house is like Toddler Disneyland where rules and sugar limits don't apply.

Once upon a time if you told your mum, 'I'm hungry', her response would have been, 'get an apple'. But with your kids it's 'Did you want some chips? Some biscuits? I bought a nice cake at the shops today!'

Sure it would be nice if they didn't spoil them quite as much, but then again, how lucky are kids to have grandparents in their lives? How special to have more adults to love them and dote on them like the little masterpieces they are. Grandparents are golden, but especially in toddlerhood when kids start to get a little bit tired of hanging out with their parents. They've reached the age when they want to broaden their social circle a bit. Preferably to include those lovely old folk whose eyes light up when they walk through the door and who say yes to every frivolous demand thrown at them. Which is a little bit rich, considering how strict they were with you.

Watching my parents with my kids is one of the great joys of my life. Knowing how much they adore them and worry about them makes me feel like I have a team. And my children would drop me in a heartbeat if there was ever an option to go and live with Nanny and Papa. They're just more fun than I am.

# 112

# The too-fun mum

. . . on the other hand, is a disaster.

For babies it's a disaster because they'll get all hyped up and they'll look like they're having a grand old time until suddenly they're not and their heads start spinning and they start screaming like they're being gutted. This is called being 'overstimulated and overtired' and it's not ideal.

A toddler is better equipped to cope with all the excitement of play and noise, but it's at your own risk.

The trouble with toddlers is: they have the endurance of an iron man on speed. They will happily play the same game over and over and over again until you feel hot tears of despair spill down your face. So you have no one to blame but yourself if you make the mistake of being dangerously fun and entertaining. An experienced parent would never do this.

This is why parents are all sitting down, drinking wine and telling the children to go and entertain themselves. It's not because we hate our kids, it's because we don't want to get stuck playing the same fecking game for an hour. It's not laziness, it's *strategy*.

# 113

# The witching hour(s)

It is the great divide between those with kids and those without. The witching hour(s).

Before you had kids, you probably spent the hours between 4 p.m. and 7 p.m. wrapping up a few things at work then heading home for dinner, or perhaps out to meet up with friends for a jolly laugh and a beverage or four. You may have looked forward to seeing your partner and having an intimate chat about your day, international politics and your life dreams. Your day was done and you were ready for some fun. The biggest wrinkle in your afternoon was battling the traffic to get home.

Now you're engaged in a completely different battle. You are battling the desire to just walk out the front door and not come back. There are infants battling wind, colic and exhaustion. There are toddlers battling EVERYTHING.

The baby refuses to exist anywhere but on her mum's hip and will claw handfuls of thigh flesh in an attempt to scale Mount Mum, whingeing and whining all the way to the top, where she wails non-stop from 4 p.m. until 7 p.m. The toddler insists on opening every cupboard and drawer in the kitchen so he can throw every item he finds on the floor to create a fun obstacle course for anyone carrying pots of scalding water.

Childfree people will sometimes catch a glimpse of this alternate universe when they make the mistake of calling their friends with kids during the witching hours.

It's a glimpse into a horrifying, face-melting scene of roaring terror that makes them wish they'd never picked up the phone. The call is, at most, two minutes long, in which approximately three sentences are spoken, in between yelling and shrieking and crashing and swearing, followed by the phone being dropped on the floor and kicked under the couch while the poor innocent caller is left crying, 'Hello? Hello?' into the abyss before hanging up, fed-up, forlorn, forgotten.

Things get ramped up to Factor FML when Dad walks in the door.

The only intimate moments in this home will be the silent nod one parent gives when the other holds up a bottle of wine. Their shared life goal is 'bags not doing bath time tonight'.

Of course, the witching hours do end. It's a bare-knuckle, knock-down, drag-yourself-over-the-line-with-bloodied-fingernails race, but you all get there in the end.

After the longest few hours of your life, the little people—all clean and smelling fresh—wrap their sleepy little arms around your neck and instantly you panic about how fast it's all going.

# 114

# I see you

*To all the witching hour mums,*

*It was one of those evenings where I wondered for the 875th time how far my voice carries and if my neighbours had picked up the phone to call child services yet. I was faced with the world's worst toddler determined to break my spirit, and a four year old with a new-found disdain for my existence and the banality I call 'conversation'. They were screaming in tandem with a mix of rabid starvation and criminal neglect because I wouldn't play with them and cook at the same time.*

*But just as I was on the verge of placing my head THROUGH the wall of my kitchen, I smiled because I knew I wasn't alone. YOU were with me.*

*At that moment, there were toddlers across the country, thrashing on the kitchen floor, enduring the torture of not being picked up. There were preschoolers whingeing without pause, in a way that was making their parents want to push their own eyeballs right into their skull until they* could see the faint memories of the days when 5 p.m. meant sitting in the pub with friends.

I know I wasn't the only one who put the water on to boil, then ran to put the towels in the dryer, popped in a quick load of whites, ran back to the kitchen, picking up the tsunami of junk that just won't stay IN ONE ROOM FOR GOD'S SAKE, IT'S ALL I ASK, then went to wash some dishes, got the 912th request for food and realised I hadn't put the pasta in the water.

I know I wasn't the only one wondering why there has never been an award for cooking while holding a tantrumming toddler because it's a goddamn gold-medal-worthy skill.

I know I wasn't the only one wondering if 'driven insane by whining' is a legit legal defence and if crime rates are higher at dinnertime.

Thousands of whingeing toddlers. Thousands of nagging pre-schoolers. Plus all those screaming babies and whining schoolkids and sulking teens. And thousands of mums wishing someone would notice they are working their arses off.

I notice. I see you. Like, not peering through your windows or anything, but I know you're out there doing the same slog, at the same time, just like me. And that's a pretty cool feeling.

Love Lauren xx

# 115

# Food haters

Let's be clear on what a fussy eater is.

If your child has refused a meal now and then, they're not a fussy eater—they just didn't want whatever you'd dished up. If your child has been off food for a week, they're not fussy—they're probably feeling sick. If your child always refuses to eat broccoli, they're not a fussy eater—they just don't like the taste. I don't like coriander. Doesn't make me fussy, it just makes me right.

A fussy eater will refuse ALL food. It's not an aversion to a handful of flavours, it's ALL of them. Their list of acceptable foods can be counted on one hand. My son kicked and screamed when I tried to give him ice cream once. ICE CREAM.

A fussy eater WILL go hungry. They'll happily starve themselves if it means not gagging down the food in front of them. So telling them 'This is all that's on offer, young man!' makes no difference. When you say, 'There's nothing else until breakfast' they don't think,

'Hmm, that's a good thirteen hours of no food. I might get hungry tonight—better dig in!'

Parents of fussy eaters do all the things that parents of wonderful eaters think they're so clever for doing. We offer a variety of healthy foods. We don't give in and make second dinners. We don't argue and yell and make dinner a battleground. But sometimes it doesn't work, and it's got nothing to do with the parent and everything to do with the child.

Some kids are simply wary of anything new. Some kids have serious sensory issues and providing a 'wide variety of healthy foods' isn't going to change a frigging thing.

A fussy eater is a kid who refuses to venture beyond the beige diet for months. Maybe years. It's not a phase—it's a sustained campaign of hate against sustenance and it's stressful AF. You worry your child isn't eating enough and that they're going to waste away on a diet of air and toothpaste. You overanalyse everything you've ever fed them and at what point you got it wrong. And it makes it bloody hard when people judge you for not 'getting it right' when all you do is TRY. Some children simply WON'T EAT.

And please don't forget, those toddlers who just lurve sashimi and chicken pho? Yeah, plenty of those kids have turned into preschoolers who survive on a diet of nuggets and sauce. Because children are masters at changing their minds.

| | |
|---|---|
| TODDLER | Did you make this pasta? |
| PARENT | Yes. |
| TODDLER | Did you make it with love and care? |
| PARENT | Indeed I did. Much love and care. |
| TODDLER | Did you make sure it was healthy as well as delicious? |
| PARENT | It will help you grow up big and strong. |
| TODDLER | I don't want it. |
| PARENT | But you loved this yesterday! |

| | |
|---|---|
| TODDLER | That was yesterday. This is today. |
| PARENT | It's your favourite! |
| TODDLER | I think you're confused. Pasta is my favourite. |
| PARENT | THIS IS PASTA! |
| TODDLER | No. This is PASTA. I only like pasta. It shows a serious lack of self-awareness and knowledge of your offspring when you don't know the difference. |
| PARENT | EAT YOUR DINNER. |
| TODDLER | Sure, yell at me. That always works. Why don't you try some bribery next? Begging is funny too. |
| PARENT | PUT IT IN YOUR MOUTH. |
| TODDLER | It's too hot. You are trying to burn me. My mouth is melting. I have third-degree burns. |
| PARENT | Blow on it. |
| TODDLER | Oops, now it's too cold. Can't eat it. Soz. |
| PARENT | *sips gin* |

# 116

# Bath time is wet

And, after you survive dinnertime, it's bath time.

CHILD    I see it is bath time. Would you like me to take all of this water in the bath and relocate it to the floor?

MUM    I would not like you to do that.

CHILD    Are you quite sure about that?

MUM    Very sure, yes.

CHILD    I'll just put some of the water out there right now because I feel like you don't understand what I'm offering here.

MUM    I understand perfectly. Please stop.

CHILD    No, but I meant so much more than that. Like this. See how it looks now?

MUM    Stop. Stop it immediately. I mean it.

CHILD    Perhaps just a little bit more.

MUM    What is wrong with you? I said stop.

CHILD    I don't think you did.

MUM    I absolutely did. Stop right now.

CHILD     Wait, just a little bit more.

MUM       GET OUT OF THE BATH.

CHILD     Why?

MUM       I told you to stop splashing.

CHILD     Oh, did you? I must have misunderstood. I thought you meant to splash more. Like this.

MUM       *sips gin*

# 117

# Is anyone sleeping yet?

You know back in the day, when you thought you'd definitely be getting a full night's sleep by now? Ha ha, good times.

A toddler looks at bedtime with a glint in the eye. It's a challenge to be met, and tiredness is no barrier. Just moments ago he was nodding off in the bath and now that it's officially bedtime, he's doing high kicks and singing *The Greatest Showman* soundtrack, complete with laser show and elephants.

Bedtime is when toddlers move from casually insane to clinically psychopathic. Their determination to not sleep gives them the strength and kicking ability of a roid-raging kangaroo who has decided that now is the time to practise backflips, start an abstract mural on the bedroom wall and assess the cuddling qualities of every soft toy in the house. The more tired they are, the more stuff they will destroy, including your will to live.

Toddlers have an expert level ability to find reasons they can't be asleep right now:


Too thirsty

Too cold

Too hot

Need a kiss

Need a cuddle

Need to tell you somefing . . . hello

Need that coin you gave me that's now inside my piggy bank

Need a song

Need new pants

My socks are wrong

Need to see what your bed looks like because I forgot

Need to go to Nanny's house NOW

Need to speak to Nanny about your refusal to take me there. Does
    she know?

Knee is sore

Hair is sore

I am a cat now

Miaow

I didn't do a dance yet

You're my best friend, Mummy

Am I your best friend?

What is my foot called again?

Why is it called a foot?

Are you angry, Mummy?

Why?


It can become a battle and it might make you react . . . poorly.

    One night, as I lay down with my son and whispered sweet

words to him about how safe and loved he was, he turned and whispered, 'I want Daddy.'

I told that ungrateful son of a bitch (me) that Daddy was unavailable #untrue.

He leapt out of bed and headed for the door.

I stood up and, with the reflexes of a jungle cat and the legs of a giraffe, I kick-boxed that door shut over his head.

He tried for the door again and I told him he had two choices: he could lie down and go to sleep, or he could touch that bloody door and not go to his friend's party the next day #seemedfairatthetime.

He turned and roared in my face like a lion that'd just been kicked in the coit.

I pushed him out the door myself and bid him good day.

The next morning, with the backbone of a jellyfish, I drove him to that party like we both knew I would.

# 118

# And they're asleep

Even if it took 3 hours and 23 minutes, the second your child falls asleep you will remember every little thing you love about her.

Even if she slapped you clean across the face as she was lowered into her bed, the love will burst out as soon as she shudders into slumber.

Then you will regret every harsh word, every deep sigh, and every hissed threat through clenched teeth. You will punish yourself for being a failure. *Again.* Your heart will ache with remorse about another day wasted, another day when your precious child didn't get the best from you.

You will beat yourself up for all the things you did wrong but you won't spare a thought for all the things you did right.

Like all the cuddles you gave, the kisses and 'I love you's. The dance party you threw when everyone was losing it that afternoon. The way you calmed down the seventeenth tantrum of the day with patience and love. Sure, the first sixteen didn't go to plan, but you improved, right? You made the food, you cleaned the child and you were there, by her side, all day long—showing up, doing the slog, being the mum. Well done you.

And now, as your reward, you get to collapse on the couch, pour yourself a drink and watch TV/scroll Instagram while pretending to engage with your partner until you absolutely cannot keep your eyes open any longer because you've been ready for bed since 6 a.m. but you can't waste even half an hour of child-free time at night. That would just be ungrateful.

Besides, getting into bed and closing your eyes is the international code for: 'Wake up, Mummy is lying down, get into her bed now. Don't forget, she loves it when you lie across her face.'

# 119

# The grief of motherhood

Even after the hardest days, it's entirely possible to grieve a child who is standing right in front of you.

It's a bittersweet agony of motherhood that no one warns you about: the ever-present grief as you watch your child grow up—and away—from you, becoming a whole new person, over and over again.

Looking back at photos and videos causes a physical ache in your heart as you try to accept that the little one in those images is never coming back. You will remember the sound of her voice, the feel of her body in your arms, the chubby fingers and round baby face. You will remember the love you felt when you watched her sleeping face that would steal your breath away, leaving you clutching at your chest.

That's not the child you have in front of you. You now have someone new. A child you love just as much—probably even more. But nothing can erase the love you felt for the baby in those photos.

And as you grieve for the child in the photos, you look at the child in front of you and you will grieve for her too because you know that any day now, she'll be gone. She'll be so changed that this child will exist only in your heart and on your camera roll.

Soon she'll be as tall as you; she'll be kissing you on the forehead and walking out the door and you'll be aching for the little girl standing in front of you right now. And there's nothing you can do to stop it.

Every day you'll want to go back, just for a moment, just to hold that baby in your arms one last time, to remember the weight of her on your chest. You'll try to memorise exactly how it felt to look at that little face. And sometimes the pain of it all will paralyse you.

Because even when it has been the hardest of days, you will still feel like it's going too fast and no matter how much you want it to slow down, it'll be over before you're ready.

And this is the greatest hardship of motherhood.

This is the price we pay for loving them so much.

# 120

# Now you are a mum

The toddler years are when you truly become a mum.

It's easy to love a newborn in all their squishy helplessness. And it's easy to love a baby, with those big bright smiles, those pudgy, clapping hands, and those delighted gurgles every time you walk in the room.

A toddler is . . . a challenge. A toddler tests you every day to see how far your love can be stretched.

How far? The answer is: to the moon and back. Because your love is greater than anything a toddler can throw at you.

Even when she's kicking and screaming, and you're wishing she was still the happy, clappy baby you used to know, your love won't lessen. You might even love her *more*.

You pass the test every day, even when you lose your cool and want to hitchhike to Byron Bay and become a street performer for spare cash. Even when you climb into the laundry cupboard and call your mum to sob about how horrible your child is. Even when you lose all sense of reason and scream at your beloved child, only to be felled by the tidal wave of guilt as soon as the words leave your mouth. You just keep passing the test. Your love never fades.

Because toddlers are *life*—from their crazy bed hair down to their stubbornly bare feet. Toddlers are at the very edge of becoming people and they'll reflect everything that's right and wrong with the world in the space of an afternoon.

You'll never feel more like a mum than when you have a toddler. From the moment they wake you up to the moment they finally pass out, they'll keep you on your toes with pure joy, guaranteed chaos and endless laughs.

You'll spend the day kissing imaginary injuries, conversing with stuffed animals, negotiating hostage situations, teaching manners, singing songs, wiping bottoms, drying tears, picking food up off the floor, enforcing rules, witnessing new skills, clapping impromptu dance recitals, chasing runaways, commentating your own poo break, trying to say no in creative, non-confrontational ways, and hugging. Lots of hugging.

Some days will be sunshine from start to finish. Some days will be mass panic and confusion.

They'll push and push until you're falling to the rocks below, and then they'll do something so loveable, so brilliant, so irresistible that you'll float.

So you keep showing up. You keep loving this child of yours. You are the best mum you can be, every damn day, because you wouldn't want to do anything else.

True love isn't when you love someone for all their good qualities; it's when you love them despite their bad.

Even if you didn't have to, even though it's hard, you'd still choose to be a mum. And that, right there, is unconditional love.

# Part five
# Beyond

*Dear Mum,*

*It. Gets. Better.*

*People don't say this enough. They prefer to terrify mothers with the old, 'Just you wait until \*insert obnoxious behaviour here\*' any time you complain about your little one. They desperately want you to know you've got it easy and kids just become more and more horrible as they get older.*

*Listen to me: it gets better.*

*Other people will become far less interested in your kids; absolutely no one cares what your six year old is doing at school. Six year olds don't impress everyone with their completely generic achievements.*

*But they'll impress YOU. You will grow more and more proud of your incredible creation every day. You'll be blown away with just how smart and insightful they are. Kids are crazy clever. They see things we don't see, and they interpret life in such a beautiful way it'll make you sad you ever grew up.*

*JUST YOU WAIT . . . Wait until your four year old turns around and tells you, unprompted, how beautiful you are. Or your five year old tells a complete stranger how funny his mummy is. Or your six year old sits there and ponders the meaning of life in such a profound way you pick up your phone to call MENSA because it's clear you've raised a genius.*

*Yes, kids become more complicated—no question. The mental load of raising them gets heavier and heavier. Navigating their emotions, their sense of self, their self-confidence, their relationships with other people . . . it's intense and hard for everyone.*

*But* the grind *eases. The physical toll lessens. They won't need you every second of every day. You'll be able to have your own time, your own space and your own thoughts. They'll dress and feed themselves, they'll find their own entertainment, you won't need to watch them every minute. The rewards will outweigh the effort, by far.*

*Your child will still challenge you, and you'll work harder than you've ever worked to help him through it. And then, one day, when you see him achieve something you didn't dare dream would happen, the pride will flood your entire body until it leaks out of your eyes.*

*It might be something so minor that no one else even blinks an eye, but YOU'LL KNOW what it means. YOU'LL KNOW how many nights you lay awake fretting. YOU'LL KNOW what it took for him to do that tiny, insignificant thing and you will feel like it's the greatest accomplishment of your life because you helped him do it.*

*That's the kind of reward I'm talking about. And those little moments will happen more often than you think.*

*Yes, lots of it gets harder. Lots.*

*No one ever tells you the ache you'll feel as you wave him goodbye at school; the pain drowning you as you walk away, because you're leaving him to become his own person without you watching.*

*No one tells you the rage you'll swallow when you see another kid say something awful to your baby, knowing you have to let her deal with it because, actually, she's not a baby anymore.*

*No one tells you how shockingly hurtful your child can be to you. When they say awful things on purpose because they want to hurt your feelings, it'll wound you more than you'll know.*

*No one tells you how agonising it is to see your child struggle with something and not be able to fix it for him instantly. You'll literally hurt with wanting to make it better.*

*No one tells you how ANGRY you'll feel at the world—the pure, white-hot fury at how effed-up the whole planet is and how violently you want to fix it because your child needs to live here and it's just not up to scratch.*

*No one tells you that all of this will change you. Over the years, you'll realise you're nothing like the person you were before you became a mum. It happened slowly. Like a cliff eroded by waves, you've been stripped back and shaped by the constant crashing of responsibility, love and worry.*

*But it's okay. I think you'll like the new you. She'll be stronger and softer all at once; she'll be motivated and focused like never before; she'll be stressed and burnt-out. But she'd never go back.*

*Oh, Mumma, you're in for such a ride. You won't ever regret stepping on board.*

*Love Lauren xx*

In raising my children, I have lost my mind but found my soul.

—Unknown